The
❦ Deluxe ❦
Transitive Vampire

The Deluxe Transitive Vampire

The Ultimate Handbook
of Grammar for the
Innocent,
the Eager,
and the Doomed

Karen Elizabeth Gordon

Pantheon Books New York

Library of Congress Cataloging-in-Publication Data

Gordon, Karen Elizabeth.
   The deluxe transitive vampire : the ultimate handbook of grammar for the innocent, the eager, and the doomed / Karen Elizabeth Gordon.
       p.   cm.
   Enl. ed. of: The transitive vampire, © 1984.
   Includes index.
   ISBN 0-679-41860-1
   1. English language—Grammar—Handbooks, manuals, etc.
I. Gordon, Karen Elizabeth. Transitive vampire.   II. Title.
PE1112.G578   1993
428.2—dc20   92-50784

Book design by Fearn Cutler & Laura Hough

Manufactured in the United States of America

19 18 17 16 15

Dear Reader:
This book is
for you

❦ Contents ❦

🌱 Acknowledgments 🌱

THANKS
    to my brother, Bruce, for too much too soon,
    and leaving me some mischief for later

Dale Blagrave and Milo Radulovich for putting me in my
           place
La Bou for another one to run off to

BRAVO and Global Beat
Copies Now for copies then

John Grafton and Dover Publications have been most
           generous.

MORE THANKS:

Patti Fairbrother, Denise Spisak, and Camilla Collins for
groundwork and footwork, and to Camilla for noting the
           flasher

Barrie Maguire for letting his political skeleton out of
the closet so he could expose himself to a participial
           phrase

Technological translation: Curt Kurokawa

Epifanie Dadamogia, aka Fany Darzins, on bouzouki and
sewing machine

Fearn Cutler has been quite the resilient trooper
through the awkward and ultimate stages of design.

For the bestiary: Kay Locke and
Catherine Maclay Schoch

Nostalghia: Boris Lopatin

For constancy and curiosity, indulgences and visions:
Charles Mitchell, Jann Donnenwirth, Caroline
Sinavaiana, Tim Becher, Holly Johnson, Fred
Guenzel, and Linda Parker-Guenzel

For the beginnings:
Carol Dunlop, Julio Cortázar,
Kay Turney, Elisabeth Scharlatt

For ever after:
Drago Rastislav Mrazovac

THANK YOU!

Grace Fretter for the stairways and silences
Lisa Weber for slow dances and tangos

Inspiration and affinities: Ornella Volta, Charles Simic,
Sunny Smith
and
Heartthrob:* Youssou N'Dour

Muse: Silvia Monrós-Stojaković

Merci mille fois
       à Danielle Mémoire et Guillaume
       Pineau
       des Forêts for the deus ex machina,
       bathtub, and castle
       to Pat Nolan for moon stanzas and
       my grandfathers

For masterminding, and tripping through the treachery:
Maia Gregory

For her part in this: my editor, Shelley Wanger

For my mother, Camilla Collins, aka Honey Hall:
       Boundless thanks for the mystery of life
       for rules to baffle me
       for devotion beyond the call of childhood

* See Verbs.

Maureen Jung,

Editorial wizard and ethereal body guard,

I thank for arriving, with the gold rush, to map this troublesome terrain, survey the cacophonous subject, and make me stick to it, wolf packs and all. My parallel playmate at La Bou, Maureen charted her gold miners and mule teams while I courted gargoyles, fed mastodons with marzipan, chased a rabbit on flying horseback, loaded the rats' revolver, coupled a debutante with a troll, and plotted the liberation of a trapped body and soul. These stories came flapping into Maureen's computer on battered pages and emerged a lavish manuscript the printer surely kissed in secret, so truthfully was everything in place. I shall be undyingly grateful to Maureen, also, for keeping me away from Procrustean bedfellows, taxidermists and taxonomists, and occasional ravenous doubts.

Irene Bogdanoff Romo,

Adopted sister and illumination assistant,

entered into this otherworldly frolic to complement my rapt and rampant visions with grace, skill, fidelity, and patience, adding her laughter to the menagerie that multiplied from one chapter to the next. Irene helped turn my beastly and erotic confections into camera-ready perfections, and my slapdash studio into a blazing production wing. Together, we added locks and doors, hands, clouds, and seashells, arrows, faces, and hearts; drew the feline ex machina's bath; and furthered, finned, and feathered these stories along their madcap way.

🌿 Preface 🌿

It is in high spirits that this opulent, rapturous, vamped-up grammar drama leaps into your lap. Thanks to readers of its older sister, this one *had* to happen, and not at all quietly. Howling, exploding, crackling, flickering with new life-forms, and drunk on fresh blood (some of mine is certainly missing), this deluxe edition reminds us on every page that words, too, have hoofs and wings to transport us far and deep.

Protagonists like Timofey, the lamia, and the little maestro have been joined by other shady characters: Even the sun is looking suspect. A gang of rats has entered the fray, and a horse thief on rabbit paws. Dope fiends and gargoyles and wild-eyed women show their faces as never before. Mog Cinders is still hunting butterflies, but this time we see her methods — as magical as the way sentences appear from who knows where (and you *will* know where before we're through). The vampires have multiplied, toting family values and other household items in their coffins of earth. Alyosha has intensified (dare I say consummated?) her attachment to one gargoyle in particular, who initiates us into the most basic components of a sentence as we wade into his life. Attachments are what this book is all about: not so much rules to learn and break as relationships, myriad combinations through the alluring guises that haunt most words and attract them to one another.

The debutante who had taken her haunches from the

ballroom to ponder her meaningless life is now jabbering her heart out to a troll; as intrigued as we were with her dark night of the soul, the troll has set the scene so confidences would flow. But the dance does go on — an endless tango swirling and kicking, about-facing all over the floor. A podiatrist is on hand, keeping everyone's feet and hoofs in terpsichorean shape. And a runaway from *The Garden of Earthly Delights* reminds us now and then that reading is one delight that won't abandon us.

But now I can no longer put off *my* confession. The truth is I have more in common with the gargoyles (monsters made useful) or Mog, or the protagonist in prison (and her counterpart on flying horseback) than with the language authorities I share shelf space with in bookstore reference sections (me and the boys). *That* is why, more explicitly than in *Vampire I*, we meet the monsters of grammar head-on, rub their horns, writhe against their shaggy pelts, tug their tales, and take them home. This time I approached the subject with more fear and trembling (awestruck at the reckless tumble it could easily turn into), and became any bemused reader/writer hoping for illumination. Each bewilderment gave me my direction in assembling and generating the text. I *crawled* beneath the lines of the previous version and found what had been left unsaid because of questions I hadn't asked. The answers came in many voices, with me emerging somewhat battered and bruised from the adventure (and there are these curious marks on my throat), but that's what it took to tear the terror from this terrain.

There's another exciting new character in all this: *you*. The ample margins invite your own pawprints so that as *The Transitive Vampire* roams this earth, no two copies will be the same. And why confine it to writing when we just want to play? Parlor games, for instance, with neth-erworldly beasts lurking in docile attitudes beneath the overstuffed chairs — stuffed with shredded Procrustean grammar texts, of course.

❦ Introduction ❦

*Like everything metaphysical the harmony between thought
and reality is to be found in the grammar of the language.*
Wittgenstein
Zettel, 55

It is not often that circumstances force me to utter more
than one sentence at a time, or, for that matter, one after
another — the usual arrangement of such things. And we
are dealing with usual arrangements here: the form and
ordering of words, be they mumbled, bellowed, or in-
scribed. Grammar is a *sine qua non* of language, placing
its demons in the light of sense, sentencing them to the
plight of prose. Don't take an immediate and sullen dis-
like to this book or look askance before you've even
begun. Do not mangle it yet. By allowing yourself to be
misled by the subject you will end up more intimate with
the knowledge that you already possess.

This is a dangerous game I'm playing, smuggling the
injunctions of grammar into your cognizance through a
ménage of revolving lunatics kidnapped into this book.
Their stories are digressions toward understanding, a
pantomime of raucous intentions in the linguistic labyrinth. By following them through this rough and twisting
terrain you will be beguiled into compliance with the
rules, however confounding those rules may appear to
be. Learning is less a curse than a distraction. If you

nuzzle these pages with abandon, writing will lose its terror and your sentences their disarray. I am not trifling with your emotions, nor flapping an antic mirage in your face. Whether you dawdle or maraud your way through these pages, you will return to them repeatedly to find your place and see your face.

Before I leave you in the embrace of the transitive vampire, I should introduce him to you, for he too went through the dubious process of education and came out none the worse for wear. He was not always a vampire. He can recall the bittersweet pleasure of a morsel of marzipan dissolving on his tongue and earlier memories of the vanished bliss of his mother's breast. He was a child of immense generosity and voracious intellect. By the age of ten he had read all of Tolstoy and Pushkin and *The Torments of Timofey*, a neglected Slavic epic that greatly affected his sensibility and filled his young mind with dread. He knew suffering from inside out, abjection like the back of his hand, which was slender and silken and thrilling to all who were touched by him.

When his manhood set in, our hero set out from home to seek his fortune, or at least his way. The mountains of his mother country were monstrously metaphysical. Words reposed in stones, and it was here, high above the cradle of his childhood, that his nature and purpose revealed themselves, not far from the howling wolves. No one knows quite how it happened, but he came back decidedly changed, transfixed through some secret effect. He had become one of night's creatures, with a grammar he had received from the great and jagged unknown. Treading carefully among the broken rules, he returned to set things straight. It was a noble undertaking, and it was noted in his epitaph, although he is immortal, like language itself, and still prowling around.

The
Deluxe
Transitive Vampire

❧ Sentences ❧

The Subject

The subject is that part of the sentence about which something is divulged; it is what the sentence's other words are gossiping about.

> *My name* is Jean-Pierre.
> *The girl* is squatting under the bridge.
> *The girl squatting under the bridge* is a debutante.
> *The door* opened.
> *The contraption* shut.
> *He* was caught.
> *His huge, calm, intelligent hands* wrestled with her confusion of lace.
> *The werewolf* had a toothache.
> *The afflicted fang* caused him to wince pathetically as he stifled his sobs in his sleeve.
> *The persona non grata* was rebuked.
> *The door* slammed in his flabbergasted face.

The *italicized* words in the above sentences form the complete subject. The simple subject, a noun or pronoun, is the essence lurking at its center, without which the complete subject would be nothing at all. In the sentences below, only the simple subjects are italicized.

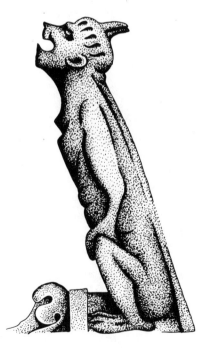

My name is Jean-Pierre.

3

My *name* is Jean-Pierre.
The *painting* leered.
The *prince* demurred.
The *innuendo* flying over her head was a
   come-on.
It landed in the fountain after dark.
A *morsel* of humility would help.
The sprightly *lummox* faltered

The Predicate

The predicate is the other necessary part of the sentence, the part that has something to say about the subject, that states its predicament.

My name *is Jean-Pierre.*
Torquil and Jonquil *plotted their tryst.*
The debutante *is squatting under the bridge.*
The werewolf *had a toothache.*
The door *slammed in his flabbergasted face.*
The vampire *began to powder his nose.*
The contraption *shut.*

The complete predicate of a sentence consists of all the words that divulge something about the subject. Like the complete subject, the complete predicate has an essence, a fundamental reality, called the simple predicate, or verb.

My name *is* Jean-Pierre.
The debutante *is squatting* under the bridge.
The werewolf *had* a toothache.
The door *slammed* in his flabbergasted face.

The subject doesn't always precede the predicate:

There were *fifty-five lusterless vampires* dismantling the schloss.
Into the circle of blind conformists leaps *a dissident* shining with woe.

Compounds

Both simple subjects and simple predicates can be compound, which means that more than one thing is going on, or is being gone on about.

A compound subject contains two or more subjects, joined by *and, or,* or *nor,* which share the same verb, are doing the same thing, are sharing the same predicament.

> *A debutante* and *a troll* are squatting under the bridge.
> *The werewolf* or *his wife* wreaked havoc in the pantry.
> *The innuendo* and *its consequences* missed their mark completely.

A compound predicate, or compound verb, is the happy issue of two or more verbs that are joined by *and, or, but, yet,* or *nor,* and that belong to the same subject.

> We *complied* but *spat* on our captors' shoes.
> The faun *approached* and *avoided* Effie all over the forest floor.
> Mog *had* a baby and *named* her Blaze.
> She *wriggled* in acknowledgment or *writhed* in uncalled-for shame.

The debutante *squatted* and *pondered* her
meaningless life.
The baby vampire *hurled* his bottle at his nanny
and *screamed* for type O instead.
The werewolf *howled* piteously and *sought*
comfort in the lap of his wife.
His huge, calm, intelligent hands *swerved*
through the preliminaries and *wrestled* with
her confusion of lace.
It neither *soothed* the unrecorded regrets nor
averted the impending doom.
He, she, and it *surrendered* the samovar, *lost* their
patience, and *tried* to find their shoes.
The debutante and the troll *shot* the breeze,
sobbed and *shuddered*, and *bared* their souls till
dawn.

Complements

Our X-ray of the basic sentence pattern reveals one more
set of bones. The complement is the part of the predicate
that completes the meaning of the verb, carrying out its
intention, its promise, following through with its tease.
The way most sentences begin leaves them clamoring for
something more.

He keeps.   He keeps *what*?

He keeps *milk cows*.
He keeps *wildebeests*.
He keeps *his opinions on a shelf*.
He keeps *her in trinkets and furbelows*.

In each of those sentences, the complement keeps the verb engaged, telling its story, instead of keeling over without having gotten a word in edgewise.

A vampire has *supple limbs.*
Cronopios have *many quirks.*

Gargoyles spout.   Spout *what?*
Gargoyles spout *nonsense.*
                    rain.
              syllogisms.

My name is *Jean-Pierre.*
My origins are *unknown.*

❧ Words ❧

Unlike so many grammarians who have made their specialty abhorrent to us, words are more Protean than Procrustean. Supple, flirtatious, acrobatic, they change form to play with one another in myriad combinations, manifold meanings. Their interactions, positions, postures—syntax—keep them from being utterly capricious. A single sentence or idea can be expressed variously, each expression having its own emphasis and tone, its own effect on the reader.

A saunter through the dictionary shows just how polymorphous most words are, and how many roles each can play within different contexts, combinations. That *saunter* in the previous sentence, for instance, is a noun. The same idea could be expressed with *saunter* as a verb: If you saunter through the dictionary, you will see just how polymorphous most words are.

The ways in which a word functions are as intrinsic to its meaning—its ability to say what it means—as its definition, both denotative and connotative. Alone, it means little and is of little use to you. Our mother tongue, lusty and fecund, has large litters of squalling brats who are, by virtue of such birthings, social creatures, always on the verge of interacting, seldom sleeping alone.

Eager—and doomed—as words are to serve you, they want to do so in lively, dashing, dancing, swooping, curving, crossing, flapping capacities, in sense and harmony with one another. Each time a word shows its face, to countenance its fellows, new possibilities reveal themselves. Language lives, breathes, moves with you — like the beings who inhabit this book.

This changeability takes various shapes through what are called *parts of speech*. Every word is inherently at least one part of speech — its potential in life — and can often act the role of three or four different parts of speech by its behavior in a given instance. As a part of speech, a word finds further versatility through its function within a sentence, in the subject or predicate.

We really must take a saunter now and applaud a handful of these affable consorts and creatures going through their paces.

Verb:

> I *fancy* dames with broad shoulders.

Adjective:

> Her *fancy* dress showed them off to great
> advantage.

Noun:

> I therefore took a *fancy* to her.

Verbal:

> The vampire began to *powder* his nose.

Noun:

> The *powder* made him sneeze all over the
> mirror, where his face was not to be seen.

Verb:

> My horse *pants* and froths.

Noun:

> I don't always wear *pants* when I ride him.

Noun:

I get my kicks from
haunted horses.

> Timofey is more afraid of the *dark* now that he
> is dead.

Adjective:

> The *dark* side of Loona is the one he already knows.

Verb:

> When Timofey returned, he *haunted* her nightgown and the box where she kept her rings.

Adjective:

> I get my kicks from *haunted* horses.

The dark side of Loona is the one he already knows.

Nouns

A noun is a word that names a person, place, thing, or abstraction. Abstractions may include emotions, ideas, qualities, notions, wishes, passions, attributes, and other things you might grasp but can't quite put your finger on.

Person:

> ballerina, taxidermist, midwife, girl, boy, coward, alchemist, tenor, fetishist, ruffian, onlooker, impresario, somnambulist, starlet, thug, Sheridan Le Fanu, dissident, philosopher, glutton, Harpo Marx, dilettante, maestro, Mozart, necromancer, bride

Place:

> Bratislava, Alabama, Nevsky Prospekt, Kyoto, Martinique, Baden-Baden, Samoa, Omsk, Boston, Mars

Thing:

> cigar, pocket, mirror, bubble, gonad, trombone, marzipan, stalactite, toothpick, taco, shadow, scum, ivory, clock, omphalos, snow, cup, swamp, bonbon, piroshki, mosquito, ribbon, hand, haunch

Abstraction:

> finesse, ubiquity, afterlife, monogamy, volition, solitude, pleasure, fashion, xenophobia, history, horror, Cubism, silence, ethos, antiquity, repulsion, pride, chagrin, chutzpa, titillation, suspicion, wrath, revenge

Compound nouns are nouns made up of more than one word:

> razzle-dazzle, bedroom, cream puff, toothache, bubble bath, nuit blanche, she-wolf, shadowboxing, guardian angel, gun control, amour-propre, white-collar worker,

White-collar worker

dreadlocks, looking glass, mug shot, lava-lava, rite of passage, F-word, deus ex machina, tea party, Nova Gorica, clodhopper, half-truth, bodice ripper, sweet tooth, dope fiends

Dope fiends

Pronouns

Potential dope fiend

A pronoun also names, by taking the place of a noun. The noun for which the pronoun is stepping in is called its antecedent.

> *The chap with the long face* is buying *his* insurance policy.
> *The guys at the gym* were snapping *their* towels.

The girls in the corner are
waiting to do their number.

The girls in the corner are waiting to do their
  number.
There was a lull in the conversation. It was
  embarrassing.
What is the name of that surly bloke? I'm dying
  to meet him.

The pronoun stands for the other words accompanying the noun as well as the noun itself. Thus, *his* replaces all of *the chap with the long face*; *him* replaces not only the bloke but his surliness, too.

> *Our* lapses are not unconscious.
> *His* off-color bagpipes are out of tune.
> *Your* contrition is adulterated with aplomb.

The antecedent is not always stated; yes, it does come before, but often before the sentence begins. In "*I* want *my* mommy," we have the antecedent and the pronoun together, in cozy proximity. *I*, too, has an antecedent — it refers to an unnamed speaker.

Here, the antecedent *I* is understood, wild hair, distraught features, and all:

> *My* horse has disappeared.

If we have been gossiping about François, our summer houseguest from Montréal is understood as the antecedent when we say, "*He* likes marmalade on *his* tartine."

Adjectives

Adjectives, like adverbs, are modifying words. A modifying word changes, enhances, stirs, intensifies, makes more precise our concept of another word — the one (or ones) it modifies. An adjective does this to nouns and pronouns.

Descriptive adjectives describe a noun or pronoun, stating what kind of person, place, or thing either one is:

blue blood, *bashful* poltergeist, *portable* landscape, *inept* marauders, *innocent* onlooker, *Turkish* wolfhound, *mad* tea party, *sugar-coated* speech, *Italian* sports car, *Renaissance* man, *injured* appendage, *Shakespearean* sonnet, *suffering* soul, *wrong* track

He is *gorgeous*.
This is *disgusting*.
You're *sweet*.
It's *shaggy*.   .
They're *spectacular*!
Are you *alone*?

Limiting adjectives specify, quantify, or identify the noun presented.

our quesadillas
some hanky-panky
those dirty rats
much reflection
no trouble
little promise

Limiting adjectives take several different forms: possessive, demonstrative, indefinite, interrogative, and numerical. Definite and indefinite articles can also be limiting adjectives.

Possessive Adjectives:
my shyness, *his* standoffishness, *her* apprehension, *our* shame, *their* greed, *your* delusions

Demonstrative Adjectives:
> *this* contretemps, *those* rhapsodies, *that* samovar,
> *this* debutante, *those* mastodons, *that* rat

Indefinite Adjectives:
> *any* provocation
> *either* floor plan

Interrogative Adjectives:
> *which* nodule?
> *whose* xenophobia?
> *what* quirk?

Numerical Adjectives:
> *one* fin, *two* fangs, *six* senses, *three* whiskers,
> *fourth* horseman, *seventh* afterthought, *first* bra

Articles:
> *an* Anglophile, *the* promontory, *a* zipper,
> *a* welcome onslaught, *an* aphrodisiac, *a*
> codependent guardian angel, *the* chimera,
> *a* feline deus ex machina, *the* haunted horse

A Note on Placement

Although it is usually placed directly before the noun it
is describing, an adjective can also come after the predicate, connected to the noun by a linking verb, such as *be*
or *seems.*

> Dawn kissed the horizon with its *fresh, hot* lips.
> The lips of dawn were *fresh* and *hot.*

His *bleary* eyes stared back at him.

His eyes seemed *bleary* as they stared back at
him.

The little maestro jetlagged around the
Continent with his *out-of-tune* cellist and his
rowdy claque.

His cellist was *out of tune* and his claque was
rowdy.

Verbs

A verb is the momentum in the sentence. It asserts,
moves, impels, reports on a condition or situation. It is a
vital part of any sentence even though it's the subject
who is doing, acting, being, emoting. What the verb
asserts may be an action or an identity or a state of being.

Action:

The waif *whimpered*.

The onlooker *ogled*.

The aristocrat *undulated*.

The bistro *burned*.

Trinculo *drinks* a lot.

Effie *crushes* herbs beneath her pattering feet.

Effie's calloused bare feet *patter* over tender
young herbal shoots.

The lamia *put* the frog in her samovar.

State of Being:

Her fiancé *is* a somnambulist.

His dreams *are* mobile.

Her fiancé is a
somnambulist.

We'*re* new to this part of the world.
You'*re* out of your mind, you know.

Auxiliary (or Helping) Verbs:

The persona non grata *was* rebuked.
The debutante *is* squatting under the bridge.
A morsel of humility *would* help.
I *am* staying out of trouble.
He *hasn't been* seen in this restive republic for
    years.
Do you get my drift?

Adverbs

An adverb modifies — changes, enhances, limits, describes, intensifies, muffles — a verb, an adjective, or another adverb. It can also modify verbals, prepositions,
and conjunctions.

She guffawed *helplessly*.
She was *rather* helpless.
She guffawed *rather* helplessly.

He gaped *primly*.
He was *very* prim.
He gaped *very* primly.

She beckoned *crassly*.
She was *exceedingly* crass.
She beckoned *exceedingly* crassly.

He groped *hesitantly*.
He was *very* hesitant.
He groped *very* hesitantly.

Adverbs tell when, how, where, and to what extent an action is done or a state of being exists.

Time:

He came *immediately*.
I'll be with you *shortly*.
Loona lunches *late*.

Manner:

Bats walk *silently*.
The impresario was *roundly* bowled over.
He *squeakily* backtracked.
She took the palliative *sublingually*.
The orgy proceeded *parliamentarily*.

Place:

I must loiter *here*.
This is *where* I belong.
You must tarry *here* no longer.
The ubiquitous baguette was *nowhere* to be seen!
François goes *everywhere* with his tartine.

Degree:

She was *quite* inconsolable.
He was *most* invincible.
I was *very* miserable.
He was *quite* affable.
They were *very* jolly.
I did not *sufficiently* splutter with gratitude to be
    worthy of further favors.
That butterfly net is *quite* unnecessary.
It's a familiar *enough* muddle, all right.

I was very miserable.

Prepositions

Prepositions, unobtrusive go-betweens that they are, indicate the relation of a noun or pronoun to some other word(s) in the sentence.

> He slapped her *on* the scapula.
> They toyed *with* the idea amorously.
> Get *out of* that corner.
> Don't corner me *in* this one.
> I spluttered *with* gratitude.
> Lisa shakily stood her ground *with* the
>   obstreperous opposition *of* her puny will.
> We are poised *on* the brink *of* a new world
>   disorder.
> We chatted unctuously *into* our bowls *of* soup.
> The baby vampire hurled his bottle *at* his nanny
>   and screamed *for* type O instead.

> *up* the Amazon
> *with* wings *of* gossamer

Some of the more popular prepositions in our language include:

> above, across, after, along, among, around, at,
>   before, behind, below, beside, besides,
>   between, beyond, but, by, down, during, for,

from, in, inside, into, near, of, off, on,
outside, over, past, since, through, till, to,
toward, under, until, upon, with, within,
without

He reached *across* her to grab the lamb chop
asleep *in* the center *of* the table.
It used to live *near* a waterfall *under* a canopy
bed.
Within the bounds *of* propriety profligacy reigns
supreme.

Procrustean grammatical etiquette admonishes us not to
end sentences with prepositions. Certain verbs, however,
travel around with prepositions familiarly attached to
them — cuddle up, finish off, shut up, shut off, chime in,
make out, turn on, come to — and protect their familiars'
right to be there.

There wasn't a single item in my closet that I
could don with impunity, nor was there a
shoe fit to *boogie in.*

Using a demotic word like *boogie* precludes formal adher-
ence to rules, except for comically incongruous effect:

There wasn't a single item in my closet that I
could don with impunity, nor was there a
shoe in which it would be seemly to boogie.

In the fervor of a thumbnail sketch, few who'd met their
match would warble through so many syllables to pro-
nounce:

That strawberry blonde is certainly someone
with whom to reckon.

That strawberry blonde is certainly someone to
reckon *with*.

Prepositional Phrases:

A prepositional phrase is made up of the
preposition, the noun or pronoun that is its
object, and the modifiers of the object.

The debutante rocked back and forth *on her
haunches*.
They waddled *down the trail / to the ruins*.
(two prepositional phrases together)
Meet me *under the magnolia / at twilight / without
your wig*. (three prepositional phrases in
a row)
Come *to my senses* and climb *into my drift*. (two)

Compound Prepositions:

Compound prepositions, or prepositions made up of
more than one word, also scatter themselves profusely
across the written world.

apart from, as for, as well as, aside from, because
of, by means of, contrary to, for the sake of,
in back of, in case of, in front of, in place of,
in spite of, inside of, instead of, out of,
together with, up at, up to, with regard to

in front of the famous cathedral
out of the loud hound of darkness
together with unarmed citizens
instead of these mortifying dahlias
in addition to marzipan and gingerbread
in the place of Louvelandia

by means of these clumsy machinations
inside of this unblinking immobility
because of those bounced checks
apart from the rats and the horse thief

Conjunctions

Conjunctions are words that join words, phrases, or clauses, just as the word *or* in this sentence links the words *phrases* and *clauses*. Conjunctions are humble and quite useful; you might barely notice them most of the time, but if a conjunction were removed or used out of context, an awkward gap would be felt.

Since conjunctions show logical relationships (just as *since* is doing right here), they should be chosen and used with care. They may be small, but their misuse can have enormous consequences — especially when they're joining clauses. Notice their precision, and let that focus you.

Coordinate Conjunctions:
Coordinate conjunctions join words, phrases, and clauses that are of equal importance or of the same grammatical structure within a sentence. The most common coordinate conjunctions are *and, but, for, or, neither, nor,* and *yet.*

> The robot *and* the dentist tangoed beneath the stars.
> They used to meet in the parking lot *or* at a nearby bar.
> They often danced in public, *but* no one seemed to mind.

Neither his existence *nor* his vacuity betrayed his
   true intent.
Her antic *yet* coercive repartee confuted his
   dismay.

Subordinate Conjunctions:

Subordinate conjunctions usher or shove you right into
a dependent clause — one functioning, for example, as an
adjective or adverb. If a sentence begins with a dependent clause (as this one does), the subordinate conjunction (in this case, *if*) comes first, so that it can state the
condition or circumstance modifying the independent
clause. Otherwise a subordinate conjunction may come
between the parts of the sentence it connects.

If Lucifer confesses, we'll let the rest of you go.

If Lucifer confesses, we'll let
the rest of you go.

After they removed the leeches, she showed him
    to the door.
They dropped the subject *before* it got too hot.
I took an instant liking to him *even though* his
    hands were covered with fur.
If I die first, will you tuck me into my casket?

Here is something I feel I ought to warn you about. Since
a subordinate conjunction at the beginning of a clause
renders it incapable of standing alone (as the word *since*
does this one), whereas without the conjunction it could
stand alone perfectly well, you must watch out for the
ever-lurking potential of creating sentence fragments by
failing to connect the dependent clause thus established
with an accompanying independent clause.

    Not:
Well, don't get into a swelter about it. Since jeopardy
was the inevitable upshot of this stupid farce.
    But:
Well, don't get into a swelter about it, since jeopardy was
the inevitable upshot of this stupid farce.

Subordinate conjunctions include:

    until, since, if, because, after, before, although,
        that, as if, so that, though, unless, while,
        when, where, even though, whereas, in order
        that

    Since the schloss lies far to the east of our
        mother tongues, we always come with
        interpreters.
Where were you *when* the samovar erupted?

Correlative Conjunctions:
Correlative conjunctions indicate a reciprocal or comple-
mentary grammatical relationship, and include:

> either . . . or
> neither . . . nor
> not only . . . but also

Conjunctive Adverbs:
Conjunctive adverbs are adverbs that join independent
clauses, which may also be whole sentences. They include: *accordingly, afterwards, also, besides, consequently, earlier, furthermore, hence, however, indeed, later, likewise,
moreover, nevertheless, nonetheless, otherwise, similarly, still,
then, therefore,* and *thus.*

> They don't have me down as a bad person yet;
> *however*, it could happen at any time.
> There is always room for improvement;
> *moreover*, in this case that's all the room
> there is.
> She's off in the gazebo having a little crise de
> nerfs. *Nevertheless*, her eyes will be dry for the
> big shebang tonight.

Interjections

An interjection is a word or collection of words that
expresses feeling. An outcast, set apart from the other
seven parts of speech, the interjection has little grammatical connection with its neighboring words or sentences. However, since it is strong, or emphatic, it
doesn't really care.

Oh! You must meet the
children's new nanny!

Very well, I'll slick your hair
down myself.

Boo!
Ah!

Indeed, the baby vampire's gums are bleeding;
    it's not what you're thinking at all.
Well! Fancy meeting you here.
Oh! You must meet the children's new nanny!
Very well, I'll slick your hair down myself.
Dear me, what cherubic chops you have!
Goodness! What a wallop you pack!
Wow! What unattainable bliss we've nearly
    achieved!
My god! I must remember your name!

❧ Nouns ❧

As you have known for ever so long, nouns are names of people, places, things, or abstractions. A noun just is — or isn't. Even when it isn't, as when we are writing or talking about its absence, *it is*. That's the pure, simple beauty of the noun: utter the word, and you have company on your hands, however abstract (apathy, hypothesis, dissent), palpable (balsa wood, marzipan), or specific (the Loch Ness Monster, Elvis Presley, *The Duino Elegies*). The name calls it forth, even if only to send it away.

Nouns have fallen into the hands of taxonomists and have been classified. Once you know you are dealing with a noun, you can further praise its qualities and put it to use in several different ways.

Common nouns are nouns that utter the name of one or more members of a large class of things:

> rabbit, door, gin, moose, mischief maker, face, limousine, movie, girl, button, tattoo, cookie, lake, silhouette, tulip, storm, wave, trinket, cuff, clue

Proper nouns name a specific person, place, or thing:

> Dionysus, Bela Lugosi, London Bridge, Malta, Egyptology, Big Sur, Gertrude Stein,

Rabbit

30

Alyosha, Mudhead, East Seventy-second
Street, Anjula, Janáček, Satchmo, Austria,
the Berlin Wall, Oscar Wilde, Transylvania,
Tiresias, Monty Python, Mother Goose

Collective Nouns:
Collective nouns are nouns that give names to groups of
things or people:

squad, flock, luggage, herd, gang, orchestra,
mob, furniture, plethora, crowd, horde,
audience, harem, quintet, coterie, gaggle,
cluster, club, caboodle, swarm, throng, coven,
bevy, galaxy, tribe, suite, troupe, bundle

a *gang* of rats
his *collection* of handmade toothbrushes

Alyosha

Hey, Alyosha is a
boy's name!

A gang of rats

a *family* of vampires
a *gaggle* of goose steps
a *handful* of gloves

Concrete Nouns:
Concrete nouns name an object that is perceivable by the senses:

> fortune cookie, hut, goose, bog, blood, tutu, spoon, piñata, glove, phone, cream, rose, pipe, calliope, moon, harpsichord, thigh, brooch

Abstract Nouns:
Abstract nouns name a quality or idea:

> solace, havoc, mood, apathy, trouble, hunch, shame, fatigue, dismay, miasma, ardor, casuistry, ire, pathos, discretion, mourning, cosmogony, luxury, ethics, transvestism, antithesis, paradox, flummery, time

Classifications have a way of breeding confusion as well as creating order. Collective, concrete, and abstract nouns are subclasses of common nouns. I hope you understand.

Concrete, abstract, and collective nouns can also be proper nouns:

> Cubism, the Beatles, the Quartetto Italiano, Trump Tower, Taj Mahal

A noun can be used in any of the following ways: as the subject of a sentence, as a complement of a verb, as an object of a preposition, as an appositive, and in direct address.

Subject of a Sentence

The subject tells who or what did it, does it, or will do it, or reveals who or what is being talked about in the sentence. It is generally placed before the verb.

> The *water* rippled.
> *Sparks* flew.
> The little *maestro* took a bow.
> The *concert hall* crepitated.
> My *hair* crackled.
> *Torquil* and *Jonquil* plotted their tryst.
> *Rome* goes back to the wolves.
> *Effie* flinched.

Later on you will see how a verb can precede its noun.

Complement of a Verb

A word that completes the meaning of a verb in a sentence is the complement of the verb. Complements are either direct objects, indirect objects, or subjective or objective complements.

> The lamia assaulted a *baba* in red boots and demanded a *cigarette* and a *scarf*.

Direct Object:
A direct object answers the question *what?* or *whom?*
after the verb.

> I scratched the *knee*.
> He chastened *Daisy.*
> Let's just split the *difference.*
> Hold your *horses.*
> Akaky wants an *overcoat.*

The direct object may also be a pronoun.

> I scratched *it.*
> He chastened *her.*
> Let's just split *it.*
> I trade *them* for voice lessons.

Indirect Object:
An indirect object tells *to* or *for whom* or *what* the
action of the verb, however welcome or unwanted,
is committed:

> I gave the *gadfly* a piece of my mind.
> I sent *Satchmo* a billet-doux.
> The mannequin gave the *baby vampire* her
>   phone number and returned to her window
>   alone.

A pronoun can also be used as an indirect object:

> I gave *her* a piece of my mind.
> I sent *him* a billet-doux.

Subjective Complement:

A subjective complement comes hot on the heels of a linking verb to explain or identify the subject. If the subjective complement is a noun, it is called a "predicate noun."

That grande dame was once my *compatriot*.
A tingle is a *pleasure*.
That mound of dirt is her *bedfellow*.
You're really *something*.
You will be my *nemesis*.
A stepfather is a *faux pa*.
Thinking is not her *forte*.
That lummox is a *liability*.
My son is a *horse thief*.

My son is a horse thief.

Your rapture is my *anguish*.
This harangue is my *relief*.

Pronouns and adjectives can also operate as subjective complements, if you care to give them the chance:

Predicate Adjective:
> That conjuror is *droll*.
> The sunburn proved *fatal*.
> The dancer seems *antsy*.

Predicate Pronoun:
> I am positive the culprit is *I*.

Subjective complements can follow only these groups of linking verbs: forms of *to be* (*am, are, is, was, were, been, will be*); verbs of the senses (*look, hear, taste, smell, sound*); and verbs like *appear, seem, become, grow, prove, remain, turn,* and *stay* (in the sense of maintaining a continuous state).

> The tea party remains a domestic *farce* with
> passions kept on a leash.

Objective Complement:
An objective complement follows and is related to the direct object.

> The robot designated the dentist his *partner*.
> Sir Gallimauf appointed Carmilla *ambassador*.

An objective complement may also be an adjective.

The famous courtesan, Mog Cinders, was an accomplished lepidopterist, too.

Those furtive tidings made Gwendolyn *gruff*.
All this friction makes Alyosha's hands *rough*.
These teethmarks render our marriage *null* and
void.

Object of a Preposition

This is how a noun looks as the object of a preposition:

That loaded dotard lives in *squalor*.
The pendulum swung over the *pit*.
Tuck yourself in between *Mog* and *me*.
You're barking up the wrong *tree*.
He bounced the bandolina upon his *knee*.

Appositive

An appositive further identifies another noun.

The little maestro greeted an unexpected guest,
a *beast* to whom he was allergic.
Mucho Trabajo, my Mediterranean *donkey*, is
losing all joy in life.
Wolves, the *Children of the Night*, always mate
for life.
Their caper, an extravagant *interlude*, ended in
an exhausted embrace.
The famous courtesan *Mog Cinders* was an
accomplished lepidopterist, too.

Direct Address

In direct address, a noun names the person (or the creature) being spoken to.

> Remember, *sweetie*, I'm your crepuscular
>   consort, so don't bother calling me at noon.
> *Dafne*, fetch my spats.
> *Fido*, snatch her purse.
> "Well, all right, *darling*," she said in a tired
>   whimper, ambushing the look he gave her
>   with a card trick and a stunt on the flying
>   trapeze.
> Hey, *girlie*, drag your carcass over here!

Hey, girlie, drag your carcass
over here!

❧ Verbs ❧

The verb is the heartthrob of a sentence. Without a verb, a subject would be abandoned, stranded in a sentence, incapable of sensing the void. There would be nothing between words but meaningless space or a clutter of adjectives, phrases, and pronouns, and maybe something to eat, but no way to reach for it or bite it, since action and feeling are missing (why's everyone *else* having all the fun?).

It's the verb that gives the subject something to do, the object something to have done to it, the complement something to complete. It raises questions and answers them, too, occasionally in the same breath. Just as no subject can get far — or stay in the same place — without a verb, no verb can strut around without a subject, which may be announced brazenly or simply implied. Even if a sentence is one word long, as in *"Scram!"* the subject is understood to be *you*, with the verb (armless, legless, but no matter) carrying the meaning all the way to the exclamation point and into the reader's head. A verb's purpose in life is to show, tell, avow, state, imply, insinuate something about its subject.

The princess *panhandled.*
The yak *yearned.*
The mime *muttered.*
Scram!

Don't *sashay* out of here without me.
Lay off the mozzarella.

Sometimes a verb is understood:

How cagey [is] his syntax.
How fortressed [is] his thought.

Verbs have different ways of behaving in sentences, ways
to instigate drama among the sentence's other parts; and
they've been given names that reflect these behaviors,
that give us a shortcut to identifying or discussing them
from one instance to another, keeping up with the pleasure and trouble they bring whenever they come on the
scene. The presence or absence of complements deter-
mines the kind of verb a verb is — unless it is an auxiliary
verb, which pays less attention to such things. A complement completes a predication, making the predicament
whole.

Transitive:
The rat *shot* the pizza chef dead.

Intransitive:
She *shot* across the ballroom floor with her
memory on fire.

The rat shot the
pizza chef dead.

Intransitive Verbs

Intransitive verbs are capable of expressing themselves
without a complement to complete their meaning.

The chimera *coughed*!

The chimera coughed!

The soporific *succeeded.*
We *huddled* under our ponchos through the
opera in the rain.
The god *thundered.*
Havelock *blushed.*
Sophie *sulked* by the spittoon.
Nemo *slouched* past the fountain.

In the last two examples, *by the spittoon* and *past the fountain* are adverbial prepositional phrases, not complements.

Transitive Verbs

Transitive verbs are those that *cannot* complete their meaning without the help of a direct object.

We *bounced* the *idea* around the saloon.
He *yanked her* out of her tedium.
She *missed* the midnight *train.*
Alyosha *patted* Jean-Pierre's *muzzle.*
The faun *approached* the *nymph.*
The nymph *evaded* the *faun.*
Daedalus *mourned* his sunburnt *son.*
I *prefer* foreign *gentlemen.*
Do you *take* this *chimera* to be your lawfully
espoused pal?
The schloss *hosted* a *riot* of miracle workers and
stretchers of gratitude.

These classifications of verbs vary from one sentence to another, depending on how the verb is used. A few verbs (such as *ignore*) are transitive only; others intransigently insist on being entirely intransitive. The labels *v.t.* and *v.i.* used in dictionaries tell you whether a particular meaning of a verb demands an object to complete it. For instance, *approached* and *mourned* in the above examples could, in other circumstances, also be intransitive:

> As the day of judgment *approached*, we were
> covering up the wrong side of our tracks.
> Ashes clinging to their curlers, the citizens still
> *mourned.*

Transitive verbs sometimes take indirect as well as direct objects.

> He *sent* his *fiancée* a *crystal ball.*

The direct object is *crystal ball*; the indirect object is *fiancée.*

Linking Verbs:

Linking — or, to put it more explicitly, copulative — verbs link a subject with a subjective complement that describes or explains it. They, too, behave intransitively. As we found out with subjective complements, these verbs include verbs of the senses — *hear, look, taste, smell, feel* — and verbs like *appear, seem, become, grow, remain, stay, prove,* and *turn* (when they refer to a state or condition). And here they are, caught in the act of copulating in various positions:

> I *am* willing and I'*ll be* ready in a while.
> She *sounded* eager, but he couldn't *be* sure.
> They *became* restless and so they went to bed.
> He *is* my solace, although he *is* also my pain.
> Trinculo *became* her confidant as the slivovitz
> disappeared.

I am willing and I'll be ready in
a while.

Note how a linking verb sticks to its subject:

She *looked* pathetic. (linking)
She *looked* into his eyes and blinked.
She *grew* more brazen. (linking)
She *grew* her hair.
I *felt* humiliated. (linking)
I *felt* a frog in my pocket.

The chaperons *emerged* from the fracas
triumphant, while the hostess *remained*
contrite.

Auxiliary Verbs:

Auxiliary verbs are also known as "helping verbs," and
they are helpful indeed. To form certain tenses (e.g.,
progressive, present, and past tenses) and to express various shades of meaning, one or more special verb forms
may be summoned into a sentence to combine with the
main verb. These are auxiliary, or helping, verbs. The
conjunction of the auxiliary and the main verb results in
a verb phrase.

I *may have* done a few things that weren't
cricket, but on the whole I *have*n't been all
that much out of line.

He *was* wolfing down his sandwich as his paw
fumbled with her knee.

Do you have any more where that came from?

The rats, *having* heisted the Brie, went in search
of a worthy baguette.

We'*ve* got a lousy connection.

The Gordian knot I *am* cutting has me in a
tizzy.

Would you attack this zipper and get this purse
off my wrist?

I'*d* like another waiter along with the hors
d'oeuvres.

Did you get a cashmere sweater? No, I got a
cashmere life.

A man on the telephone *was* shrieking
"Mommy! Mommy!" so I delicately averted
my face.

She *used* to get loaded every night.

> I *might* be able to help you, if you *can* pick this
> lock for me.
> She *was* born hairy and screeching, and *has* been
> a handful ever since.

Sometimes one or more words may come between the auxiliary and the main verb. This happens more often than you may imagine.

> *Are* we not inadvertently *finishing* off the
> goodies before the chef returns?
> Djuna eventually capitulated after she'*d*
> grudgingly *heard* out our impassioned pleas.
> *Have* any of you *seen* my muff?
> *Had*n't she brazenly *broken* the laws of chance
> once too often for such an ingenuous
> adventuress?

 Note:

The verbs in this chapter are all so-called finite verbs. More familiarly known as verbals, the infinite verbs — infinitives, participles, and gerunds — are versatile and talented, behaving as nouns, adjectives, and adverbs. So audacious and adventurous are they that they have a chapter all their own; they also spend a good deal of time romping all over the "Phrases" chapter, and then on their way out of this book.

Tense

Verb tenses not only tell time but also indicate an action's or state's continuation or completion.

Present Tense:

> I *mope* alone. She *mopes* with others.
> Meteors *rove* the heavens.
> The debutante *rocks* on her haunches and *sucks*
> her thumb.

Past Tense:

> She *moped* in the bistro. I *moped* in my boudoir.
> I *moped* for five days straight without touching
> my gruel.
> She *fumbled* with her string of pearls.

I moped for five days straight
without touching my gruel.

Future Tense:

> She *will mope* tomorrow when the impulse seizes
> her.
> She *will remember* this dark and rollicking night
> of her soul for as long as she *shall live.*

Present Progressive Tense (action going on in the
present):

> I *am moping.*
> She *is squatting* beneath the bridge.

Past Progressive Tense (action going on in a
previous time):

> I *was moping.*
> She *was pondering* her meaningless life.
> I *was* just *minding* my own business when the
> samovar suddenly blew up.

Past Perfect Progressive Tense (ongoing action
completed before another past time):

> I *had been moping.*

Future Progressive Tense (continued action coming
up):

> I *will be moping.*

Future Perfect Progressive Tense (continued
action seen as completed before a later time):

> I *will have been moping.*

Present Perfect Tense:

> I *have moped* quite enough already for one woebegone and redundant week.

Past Perfect Tense (action completed before another past time):

> I *had moped.*
>
> I *had moped* all over the veranda before I was sent to my room.
>
> After the podiatrist *had sanded* her calluses, she clubbed him with her old soft shoe.
>
> She *had* never *pondered* anything besides her fingernails before she met the troll.
>
> Timofey *had had* premonitions of an early demise before the Grim Reaper winked and flashed his scythe.
>
> Cupidity held sway over the best minds of the country; the abacus *had ousted* the lorgnette.
>
> Suspicions began to mount on the third day, after an unidentified sequined fin *had been spotted* ploughing furrows in the new next-door neighbors' field.
>
> The news *had been* carefully *laundered* before it was aired from sea to shining sea.
>
> If you *had* not *polished* the floor, he would not have smashed his kneecaps.

Future Perfect Tense (action regarded as completed at a later time):

> By the time the Ides of March arrives, I *will have moped* for two weeks straight.

Keep track of time, and don't shift tense when it's not appropriate to the sequence of actions.

Not:

He *slapped* her on the scapula and *asks* her to grapple with him.

But:

He *slapped* her on the scapula and *asked* her to grapple with him.

Not:

She *gilded* the lily and *throws* in the towel.

But:

She *gilded* the lily and *threw* in the towel.

Number

Think of the subject of the sentence, the noun or pronoun, and use a verb that matches, or agrees with, it in number. The singular form of the verb is used when the subject refers to only one person or thing; the plural is used when more than one person or thing is referred to.

Singular:

Dafne *seems* jumpy.

Solace *soothes* the pain.

There *is* some hanky-panky going on.

There *is* a midriff beneath his paw.

The cow *crumples* her horn.

The little maestro *plays* the blues when his claque *is* out of town.

Plural:

We keep our caftans under lock and key.

The curmudgeon*s have* calmed down.

The quadruped*s are* trampling her taffeta gown.
There *are* unbeaten path*s* she longs to prowl.
The little maestro and the diva *have* a bad case
 of the blues.

Passive:

> The bum *was bullied* by the grandee.

Active:

> The nymphs *dished* it out.

Passive:

> It *was dished* out by the nymphs.

Active:

> Those nymphs sure do *know* how to dish it out!

Passive ad absurdum:

> It sure *is known* to it how to be dished out by the nymphs!

The passive voice is appropriate when the action rather than the actor is to be emphasized.

> The gadfly, *having been told off*, went running home to his mommy.
> The bat suspended from Loona's hair *was repulsed* by her Nuit Blanche perfume.
> The grandee *was berated* by the bum's adoring spouse.
> The wildebeest *was sat* in the corner beside a booted baba.
> The debutante *was arraigned* and *scrubbed* with harsh soap.
> My baby *was born* out of wedlock.
> He hasn't *been seen* in this restive republic for years.

My baby was born out of wedlock.

The cow's horn *was crumpled* by a hoof on the
   wing.
Her tutu *was tugged* on by him.

Even if this comes in the midst of a story whose focus is
on the adventures and feelings of a tutu, that tugging
loses its decisiveness when expressed in the passive voice.

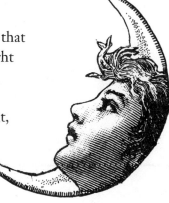

Dear Rosie and Nimrod,
   I *was left* with the many invisible things that
crawl over my body the night after the night
you were two of them.
                     Love to you both,
                     and to all a good night,
                     Loona

I *was rebuked* by a leprechaun.

Evidently the rebuke is more noteworthy than the unusual species it issues from. But in the following sentence
the passive voice is clearly overworked.

The book *was thrown* at me by them.

When the person who did it or does it (whatever it is or
was) is unknown or unimportant to the sense of the sentence, you may avail yourself of the passive voice:

The faux pas *was ignored* for several days.
Her crimes *have been absolved.*
The grub *was* grudgingly *passed* around.
The roadhouse *was ransacked* in the middle of
   the night.
The schloss *was invaded* at dusk.
The pizza chef *was found* the following morning
   with a dance card tied to his wrist.

❦ Verbals ❦

Verbals are derived from verbs, but they are *not* verbs because they do not assert anything. Still, they have been granted a half-status as *infinite verbs*—perhaps in recognition of their promiscuous availability. By their own admirable efforts in the following sentences you will see just how versatile they are. Like finite verbs, verbals may be modified and may require complements to express their meaning. Infinitives, participles, and gerunds are all verbals, each with its own purpose in your prose.

Infinitives

Hey, that's not a complete sentence!

The infinitive is a noncommittal verb form: with no inflections to show person, number, or tense, it is the verb in resting position, taking time off from running around asserting, moving, emoting, for all these nouns and pronouns. At rest, but ready to spring into action—and be conjugated—whenever a subject comes along just looking for fun or trouble. You see, it's not really all that restful: as an infinitive, a verb gets to try on someone else's clothes, act the role of a noun or adjective, or even behave adverbially with another verb that is playing its usual part. It participates in verb phrases, leading a simultaneous double life as both substantive and verb (since it can still connect with an object and be modified by an adverb).

Although the basic form of the infinitive is *to* plus the verb, there are occasions when it's unaccompanied by the *to* and is an infinitive in manner and function anyway.

> The vampire began *to powder* his nose.
> The powder made him *sneeze* all over the mirror.
> Why do you force me *to hide* your shoes?

But:

> She may *leave.*
> You must *stay.*

So let's see what this infinitive form can do to live out its limitless promise.

I want to be free.

Infinitives as Nouns:

> Sylvia loves *to split* infinitives. (direct object)
> Sylvia wants nothing except *to split* infinitives. (object of preposition)
> *To keep* a straight face in the midst of this ruckus is more than I can countenance. (subject)
> I want *to be* free. (direct object)
> Effie learned *to hide* her feelings under rocks. (direct object)
> *To find* them was the faun's most ardent desire. (subject)
> How he loved *to dangle* his participles, *brush* his forelock off his forehead with his foreleg, and *gaze* into the aqueous depths. (direct object; a triple infinitive riding on a single *to*)

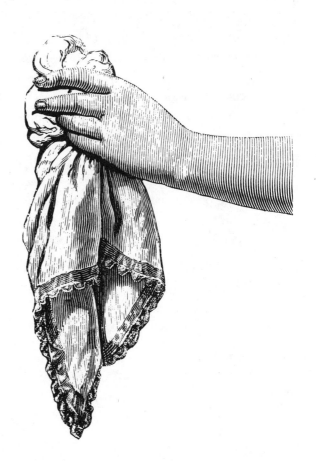

This is the hand to kiss.

Infinitives as Adjectives:
This is the hand *to kiss*. (modifies *hand*)
These are the pearls *to string*. (modifies *pearls*)
Those were the blessings *to count*. (modifies *blessings*)

These are the realities *to lament*.
Where are the days *to come*?
Such is the will *to live*.
The ubiquitous baguette was nowhere *to be seen*!
With neither friends nor foes *to hamper* him,
Timofey ties his buggy to a star.

Infinitives as Adverbs:
>Osbert was difficult *to lose*. (modifies *difficult*)
>We opened the door *to eject* him. (modifies
>   *opened*)
>He returned *to plague* us. (modifies *returned*)

>The dentist and the robot don't care *to foxtrot*.
>Her heart is easy *to break*.
>The faun was eager *to find* her.
>Doomed *to look* silly for another week until her
>   bangs began *to grow*, the lamia accosted a
>   booted baba and demanded her babushka and
>   a smoke.

Participles

Now we're encountering a beast that is so multifariously useful that it tempts you into overuse and misuse and misplacement. Participles can take the past, present, or past perfect tense, and will take on the other tenses, too:

>How *thrilling* to be here.
>I am *thrilled* to be here.
>I've never *been* so *thrilled* to be anywhere.

Past Participle:
>My bodice is *ripped*.

Present Participle:
>What a *ripping* time we had of it.

Participles function as adjectives. Present participles end in *-ing*; past participles end in *-ed*, *-d*, or *-t* or take *-en*, *-n*, or some idiosyncratic form. Both forms combine with other words to become participial phrases, which we'll later get to see going all sort of places they don't belong and creating meanings that are unintended and often comical.

> *Shedding* our pelts in the entryway, we stepped into a room ablaze with good cheer and *crackling* with come-ons and quips.

"*Shedding* our pelts in the entryway" and "*crackling* with come-ons and quips" are both participial phrases made with present participles, and act as adjectives, the former phrase modifying *we*, the latter describing the room. We could also say that the room was *blazing* with come-ons and quips, but that would be too much participial activity for one exciting sentence about to lead to much more.

The past participle can be attached to those shaggy cover-ups we were wearing only a moment before and lead us into *their* private lives.

> *Shed*, the pelts lay there quietly as our revels rocked on through the long winter night.
> The pelts, *shed* and *tossed* into a *muffled* heap, behaved with placid decorum while a cacophony of bestial bellowings proceeded in the adjoining saloon.
> *Muffled*, the pelts still managed to whisper among themselves about these disgraceful goings-on.

Present Participle:
> *Horsing* around satyrically, he leaped into her lap.

Scratching himself coquettishly, he quite won her heart.

Smiling to herself, she wondered what else he could do.

Sidling up to his mother, he asked her for a loan.

Begrudging her son his foibles, she whipped out a wad.

Clambering back to his girl, he proposed a night on the town.

Rubbing his knees together, he outlined their itinerary of dives.

Past Participle:

Flabbergasted, she acquiesced to his invitation.

Astonished, he pumped her arm.

Exhausted, she begged him to stop.

Overwhelmed, she slouched to the ground.

Puzzled, he tickled her ear.

Undaunted, she continued to swoon.

Embarrassed, he took to his heels.

Defrosted, she recovered her cool.

Present Participle:

Gyrating and *gyrating* in a widening whirl, the dancer seems the shadow of the dance.

Sitting in the nice gruff shadow of his voice, she could think of nothing to say.

The pizza chef's eyes were *bulging*, and he had a dance card *tied* (past participle) to his wrist.

missing Gorgonzola
crawling with rats

The bat suspended from Loona's hairdo was repulsed by her Nuit Blanche perfume.

Past Participle:

You won't get far in those *corrugated* pantaloons, sire.

Sylvia wantonly splits infinitives, often with *unheard-of* verbs.

The bat *suspended* from Loona's hairdo was repulsed by her Nuit Blanche perfume.

Red-booted and *seated* in the corner, Vasilisa listened to the wolves.

The wildebeest, *accustomed* to days of *unmolested* solitude, sent her R.S.V.P. with regrets.

Alyosha, *consternated* by the lichen growth on Jean-Pierre's muzzle, bought him a toothbrush and a plaque-removal kit.

Doomed to look silly for another week until her *butchered* bangs began to grow, the lamia accosted a *booted* baba and demanded her babushka and a smoke.

Past Perfect Participle:

> *Having left* her pelt in the entryway, she
>   shivered across the saloon.
> *Having been seen* ~~to have seen the crime at the~~
>   ~~scene of it, the innocent onlooker feared the~~
>   ~~rat pack would hunt her down after the big~~
>   ~~Appenzeller heist.~~
> *Having been slung* across his mother's chest
>   through infancy, the baby vampire took to his
>   hands and knees and set off into the cobwebs
>   on his own.
> A new ethos *having taken* hold of the vampires,
>   they arrived at Neptune's Playland and
>   ordered cockles and mussels and snails.

Did you say *muscles?*

Gerunds

A gerund is the *-ing* form of a verb, and it gets to live the unpredictable life of a noun, buffeted about by caprices and verbs. By now, you know that means it can be a subject, object, subjective complement, or object of a preposition.

Gerunds as Subjects:

> *Killing* time takes practice.
> *Imploring* is humiliating.
> *Lisping* is seductive.
> *Kicking* a habit takes lots of practice.
> *Practicing* demands much persistence.
> *Bumping* and *grinding* are among her many
>   fascinating tricks.

(Notice that *bumping* and *grinding* as used here are gerunds, while *fascinating* is an adjective.)

> *Sleeping* around is a thing of the past.
> *Hoping* against hope was Nadezhda's way to survive.
> *Being* both a gargoyle and an object of affection makes my existence meaningful.
> *Thinking* is not her forte.

Gerunds as Direct Objects:

> She enjoys *clapping* her tail on the rocks.
> He likes *listening* to brass and woodwind quintets.
> We enjoy *rowing* our boat through the songs of the sirens.

Gerunds as Subjective Complements:

> Her fear is *losing* control.
> His desire is *gaining* ground.
> Their nightmare is *reaching* limits.
> Their specialty is *bumping off* trolls.
> Our fear is their *mistaking* us for some.

Gerunds as Objects of Prepositions:

> By *being* so pregnant with meaning, her announcement went over like a lead balloon.
> Through *sporting* a cudgel, the Neanderthal made a rude but necessary start.
> By *dunking* her crumpet in the marmalade, Melissa committed a midafternoon faux pas.
> In *finding* the chink in his armor, she found herself shown to the door.

By confessing her culpabilities,
she cleared the way for more.

By *confessing* her culpabilities, she cleared the
way for more.
By *howling* piteously, the lycanthrope gave vent
to his pain.
The faun devoted his days to *excavating* the
landscape in search of Effie's emotions.
The goat, after *eating* her lederhosen, started in
on her Dürrenmatt.

The same *-ing* word (*yelping* and *cringing*, to take two
instances) may behave either as a gerund or as a present

participle, depending on how it is used. If you use it as a noun, it is a gerund; if you use it as an adjective, it is a participle.

> *Yelping* can be a call for help or a cry of joy.
> *Yelping* loudly, she waited for her prince to appear.

> *Cringing* is a form of self-defense.
> *Cringing* politely, he ultimately got his way.

Verbals Wrap-up: An Exercise in Distinguishing

> *Being* a waterspout and paramour keeps life *fulfilling* for me.
> The lamia has a *mottled* complexion and *flickering* tongue.
> The dentist and the robot, *following* a no-holds-barred *staging* of *Titus Andronicus*, share a vegetarian pizza with their usual beer.
> All this *huffing* and *puffing* was *bewildering* to the baba.
> If you won't refrain from *spitting* in the streets, we'll have *to send* you to Minsk via Omsk.

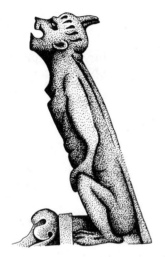

Being a waterspout and paramour keeps life fulfilling for me.

Adjectives ❧ and Adverbs ❧

While there are many ways to modify a subject or predicate, the two parts of speech in this chapter are the most easily identified and most obvious ones. Adjectives tell us more about nouns and pronouns, subjects and objects, subjective complements, appositives. Adverbs modify verbs, adjectives, and other adverbs, and occasionally even entire sentences. Adjectives and adverbs are often yawningly predictable, unmistakable, but their chapter cannot be officially declared naptime because each contains hidden terrors and possible errors, and between adjectives and adverbs lie some tricky areas where they *seem* to overlap.

Adjectives describe or limit nouns and pronouns.

> an *honest* charlatan, an *undaunted* supplicant, an *adorable* crank, a *redundant* repertoire, a *touchy* subject, a *shoddy* gag, a *supple* limb, a *red* studio, a *sulky* mood

Limiting adjectives are of various sorts: possessive, demonstrative, indefinite, interrogative, and numerical adjectives, and both definite and indefinite articles. They let us know which one, how many, how much:

> *some* stuff, *that* babushka, *two* interlopers, *this* lycanthrope, *myriad* examples, *an inordinate* amount, *an only* child

Possessive:
    their conspiracy
    our misunderstanding
    your flight

Demonstrative:
    those sea horses
    that lapsus
    these islands

Indefinite:
    any effort
    either way
    many hardships

Interrogative:
    which rodeo?
    whose handkerchief?
    what moxie?

Numerical:
    five anarchists
    third threat
    fourth floor

Article:
    an anatomy class
    a crush on him
    the staircase

Often, these limiting adjectives mingle freely among themselves as well as with descriptive adjectives.

a claptrap caboose
the inevitable crisis
the fifth door on the right
which ravaged landscape?
that charismatic Cronopio
this obsequious reply

those poor sea horses
a sleazy character
her missing tiara
those Argentine
expatriates

Nouns aren't the only words that come in compounds. Adjectives, too, can be formed through the combination of two or more words that then together modify a noun or pronoun.

a *strawberry-blond* archangel
the *monarch butterfly* migration
his *three-year* tantrum
agitprop theater
a *small-town* maestro
red licorice whips
whose *halfhearted* apoplexy?
a *double-breasted hound's-tooth* jacket

Describing, enhancing, stunning, intensifying adjectives:

a *nefarious* plot, a *rickety* garret, a *haunted* horse,
   a *lapsed* miscreant, a *botched* misdeed,
   a *throwaway* line, a *likeable* twit, a *sheepish* grin,
   unruffled aplomb, *irreconcilable* differences, a
   darling hat, a *hapless* hypochondriac, a *placid*
   ogre, a *plump* waif

My days are *endless.*
Her depths are *fathomless.*

My days are endless.

What a darling hat.

What a *darling* hat.
You're too *kind*.
The *baby* vampire is *finicky* about blood types.
Those *imponderable* looks of his are driving me
  batty.
Sometimes I prefer them, though, to a *curt* and
  cutting reply.
The little maestro, *agog* at the merchandise, lets
  rip with some expletives in French: "Dis
  donc! Sacre Bleu! Mais ouias!"

To compare qualities between two persons/things or ac-
tions/states, we have the comparative form of adjectives/
adverbs — created by adding *-er* or *more*. The superlative
comes in the same way, with *-est* and *most*.

My left horn is *more crumpled* than my right.
  (two horns)
My front left hoof is the *surest* one I've got.
  (three are in the running)

Those dahlias are *deadlier* than ink.
This acid rain is the *deadliest* we've seen yet.
Gabor played *more soulfully* today than he did
  last week.
The *most soulfully* he's ever played was on the
  night of the shooting stars.

To repeat a comparison of the more, less, *-er* type, or
the most, least, *-est* type would be superfluous. One or
the other should gush or disparage, exalt or put down,
or measure sufficiently in most matters. (Note: not *most-
est* matters, no matter how extremely you wish to emphasize the plenitude and superiority.)

Not:

This wildebeest is more swifter than that jellyfish on wheels.

But:

This wildebeest is *swifter* than that jellyfish on wheels.

Not:

That platter of tea cakes is the most creamiest I've ever seen.

But:

That platter of tea cakes is the *creamiest* I've ever seen.

Adverbs describe or limit verbs, sentences, adjectives, or other adverbs.

The somnambulist stumbled *elegantly*.
The somnambulist was *very* elegant.
He stumbled *very* elegantly.
The insomniac was *soundly* conked out.

We roughed it *begrudgingly*.
We were *awfully* begrudging.
We roughed it *awfully* begrudgingly.

They soft-pedaled the subject *ceremoniously*.
They were *rabidly* ceremonious.
They *rabidly* imposed their ceremonies.

The orchestra played *mercilessly*.
We waltzed *Lisztlessly*.

Curiously, the borzoi eschewed the bone.
Naturally, we'd prefer to take our tea in the
   cloakroom while the rest of you carry on in
   the fountain and the dark.
Unexpectedly, the aggrieving announcement
   arrived.

We roughed it begrudgingly.

She wambled *forth* and calcified.
Imponderable looks and all, he is *irresistibly*
    attractive to me.
The miscreant turned himself in *sheepishly*.
The faun is *inordinately* fond of Effie.
The hapless hypochondriac knocked about the
    world *impetuously*.
The orgy proceeded *parliamentarily*.

Adjectives and adverbs at play in the places and company
where they belong:

It is a *clinical* depression.
He is *clinically* depressed.

Her heart is *easy* to break.
She has an *easily* broken heart.

Even though many adverbs end in *-ly*, the presence of
these two provocative letters at the end of a word is not
necessarily a signal that you are staring at an adverb. Pay
attention to what the word describes, as well as how it
appears.
    Adjectives also end in *-ly* (meaning like or resembling):

sprightly, slovenly, friendly, lowly, niggardly,
    only, rascally, gingerly, unseemly, saintly,
    ungodly, lovely, unsightly, surly, comely,
    womanly, likely, stately, timely, ghastly, wily,
    ghostly, wobbly, curmudgeonly

The beauty contest was a toss-up between the
    comely contessa and the *lovely* lamia.
Those who are meek shall inherit the earth; the
    ugly ones shall have their cake and munch on
    it, too.

He is *clinically* depressed.

The wildebeest's behavior was *unseemly* when
she bounded into society, so it was not often
that she received such invitations, or accepted
them when she did.

When dressed in his most uppity drag, the
transvestite vampire appeared a *stately* damsel
all tricked out for tea.

The man in the red cape was endowed with
womanly hip sockets and forest-green eyes.

Aside from these adjectives ending in *-ly*, which do very
awkwardly at trying to turn directly into adverbs, most
adjectives become adverbs with the suffix *-ly:*

deft, deftly
neat, neatly
precarious, precariously

Some adjectives and adverbs share the same form:

only
hard
early
late

Adverbs, not adjectives, are used to modify verbs, sentences, adjectives, and adverbs.

Adverbs Modifying Verbs:

He advanced *timorously;* she quivered *enticingly.*

He pressed on *amorously;* she shuddered
voluminously.

Pauline, Josianne, and Chosette teased Jean-
Pierre *mercilessly.*

He laughed *remorselessly*; she yammered *rhapsodically*.
Rabbits reproduce *astoundingly*.

When that cat purrs *contentedly*, it feels like the end of the world.
The debutante rocked *back* and *forth* on her haunches and told the troll her podiatrist's name.

She was put sound in her place.
She was put *soundly* in her place.

The orchestra coughed concordant.
The orchestra coughed *concordantly*.

The conductor rapped indignant.
The conductor rapped *indignantly*.

She sure cut that Gordian knot!
She *surely* cut that Gordian knot!

Colloquies Among the Sybarites:
We don't always use the adverbial forms as convention and propriety dictate. It would smack of arch incongruity if Rosie and Nimrod, with sleeves rolled up, sea juices dribbling over their chins and salting their exposed midriffs at some seafood shack on the Gulf, were to exclaim to each other, "These crawdads surely do have good muscle tone!" Now, really, there are times when "They sure do" is more apt, no matter how surely you believe that it's incorrect.

Adverbs Modifying Sentences:

Inexplicably, the muddle was familiar enough.
Imperceptibly, the room had ceased to roar.
Unfortunately, that plane to Tangier was
    hijacked, precious cargo and all.

Adverbs Modifying Adjectives:

benumbingly beautiful, *dauntingly* civil,
    pathologically domestic

a *sparsely* populated bedroom
a *singularly* unattractive border guard
a *resolutely* dynamic waddle

    Not:
I was wretched sore.
    But:
I was *wretchedly* sore.

    Not:
She was a gaudy clothed cutie.
    But:
She was a *gaudily* clothed cutie.

This machine is not *exactly* user-ingratiating.
Chaperons are *usually* unwanted.
He was *almost* beautiful — in any event, more
    than *merely* okay.
These lobster claws are *quite* challenging.
You have *such* rare blood!

Adverbs Modifying Adverbs:

Not:

He bellowed unmerciful loudly.

But:

➤ He bellowed *unmercifully* loudly.

Not:

You could have behaved considerable more scrupulously.

But:

➤ You could have behaved *considerably* more scrupulously.

Not:

He rolled right up my alley rueful fast.

But:

➤ He rolled right up my alley *ruefully* fast.

Adjectives, Adverbs, and Linking Verbs

If the modifier, whether it describes or limits, belongs to the subject and not to the verb, it is an adjective.

Dafne is *jumpy*. (modifies the noun, *Dafne*)

She looks *anxious*. (modifies *she*)

Nemo looks *cunning*. (modifies *Nemo*)

The mousse tasted *plush*. (modifies *mousse*, not *tasted*)

That serenade sounds *cacophonous*.

The schloss looks *deserted*.

The desserts at the schloss are invariably *delicious*.

If the modifier describes the verb, however, it is an adverb, not an adjective. In such cases, the verb is not a linking verb; it describes the action of the subject.

> They serenaded her *cacophonously.*
> She looks *anxiously* at the creaking door.
> He looks *cunningly* at the floor.

To recapitulate an earlier illumination: copulative, or linking, verbs connect a subject to the subjective complement. A linking verb takes a predicate adjective, not an adverb. These erotic verbs include: *to be, seem, become, turn, remain, prove, stay* (when referring to a state or condition), and verbs of the senses, such as *hear, feel, look, taste, smell.*

> Her lips felt *eager.* (subjective complement of
>   the verb *felt*)
> She kissed him *eagerly.* (adverb modifying the
>   verb *kissed*)
> Her *eager* lips kissed him. (adjective modifying
>   the noun *lips*)

> She seems *incorrigible.* (subjective complement
>   of the verb *seems*)
> She behaves *incorrigibly.* (adverb modifying the
>   verb *behaves*)

> Those rats look *culpable.*
> They looked *culpably* at their Doux de
>   Montagne.

Adjectives as Subjective Complements
> My soapbox is *precarious.*
> The sunburn proved *fatal.*
> Wolves are *monogamous.*

Robots tend to get *rusty*.
Your time sheet rings *true*.
The upshot could be *disheartening*.
The outcome may prove *discouraging*.
Their repartee turned *malicious*.
Your fingernails are *frightening*.

Beware of repeating yourself tautologically, as I am doing right now, through verb and adverb combinations that are redundant.

He did it *egregiously* wrong.

she slithered *sinuously*; he betrayed her
   perfidiously; she cried *tearfully*
he pontificated *grandiloquently*; she wambled
   woozily; it stammered *haltingly* and echoed
   resoundingly
nefariously evil, *querulously* argumentative,
   lavishly extravagant

He thought *pensively*, she malingered *listlessly*,
   and no wonder, for he was *indescribably*
   nondescript.

To avoid overuse of adverbs, consider other ways to express the basic idea or image of the sentence.

The baba sat *sulkily* in the corner.
   The baba sat sulking in the corner.
   The cornered baba sulked.
   The baba sulked in the corner.
   In the corner sat the sulking baba.

❦ Pronouns ❦

When a pronoun follows its nature and substitutes for a noun, the noun is called the *antecedent* of the pronoun. Thanks to the existence of pronouns, we are spared a soporific redundancy in literature, speech, and songs. Regard the difference:

> Columbine combed the snarls out of Columbine's hair and scrubbed Columbine's body with the loofah Columbine's paramour had given the paramour's true love.

> Columbine combed the snarls out of *her* hair and scrubbed *her* body with the loofah *her* paramour had given *his* true love.

There are nine kinds of pronouns: personal, interrogative, indefinite, relative, demonstrative, reciprocal, reflexive, intensive, and expletive.

Personal Pronouns

Personal pronouns stand in for a person or other creature or thing. Besides having number and case, as we'll soon see, they are distinguished by person: first, second, or third, depending on whether the person is speaking, the person is being spoken to, or the person is being spoken of. This applies to things as well. A thing may be mute, but it can be gossiped about.

> *Nemo* suspected that *Dafne* feared *ghosts*.
> *He* suspected that *she* feared *them*.

> *The shoes* disappeared with *the samovar*.
> *They* disappeared with *it*.

> *It* is forbidden.
> *She* is doing *it* anyway.

> Leopold's bloomers are lost!
> *Leopold's* lost *his* bloomers!
> *He's* lost *them*.

Okay, here it comes, the first of the Dread Schemata, once a dance of the upper classes in the rough terrain of Bosoxia. The intricacies of this interplay oblige us to interrupt our animation festival with a table, and then to flash to a near relative on the screen as the chapter winds up to its climactic close.

Number	Person	
Singular	*1st*	I, me, my, mine
	2nd	you, your, yours
	3rd	he, him, his
		she, her, hers
		it, its
Plural	*1st*	we, us, our, ours
	2nd	you, your, yours
	3rd	they, them, their, theirs

May *I* offer *you my* sympathy?

You may offer *it*, but *I* won't take *it*.

We all ended up somewhere with *our* various
uncertain lives flapping about *us* in tatters and
our pockets full of foreign coins.

Coming into a clearing in the forest that did not
show on *their* map, *they* tilted *their* puzzled
heads heavenward to discover a
corresponding tear in the sky.

The afternoon of a faun is not much different
from *his* morning.

We all ended up somewhere with our various uncertain
lives flapping about us in tatters and our pockets full of
foreign coins.

Interrogative Pronouns

Interrogative pronouns pose questions: *who, whom, which, what,* or *whose?*

> *Who* screeched?
> *Which* is my fiancé?
> *What* happens now?
> *Whom* did I marry?
> *Whose* are these shoes?

Don't confuse the interrogative pronoun *whose* with *who's,* the contraction for *who is.*

> *Whose* cello is that in the hallway?
> It belongs to Gabor, *who's* a friend of the
>   maestro's.

Indefinite Pronouns

Indefinite pronouns refer to no one in particular; they are noncommittal, but useful nonetheless. The indefinite pronouns are *one, someone, no one, nobody, anything, something, several, each, most, all, neither, either, another, other, both, many, few, any, some, something,* and others of this same hazy ilk.

> *One* does have one's scruples, after all.
> *Several* went to bed.
> *Few* forgive without a fuss.
> *Nobody* is to be found.
> *Everyone* has disappeared.

Few forgive without a fuss.

Relative Pronouns

A relative pronoun is a pronoun that relates to an ante-cedent (as *that* in the preceding statement relates to *pronoun*) and simultaneously joins it to a limiting or qualifying clause. The relative pronouns in common use are *who, whom, whose, what, which, that,* and the *-ever* forms: *whoever, whatever, whichever, whomever.*

This is the hoax *that* they perpetrated.

She met a sophist *who* surmised her secret.
He posits hypotheses *that* are hair-raising.
She possesses some curious organs, *which* are
vestigial.

Who and *whom* refer only to persons, who may be intelligent living beings.

That trilingual solitary to *whom* you gave the
cupcakes needs a pedicure.
He adored the debutante *who* was staring into
space.
I awaited the lummox *who* was rolling right up
my alley.
That contestant *whom* you've proclaimed the
winner is busy with her snake-bite kit.
The diva, *who* was on the skids, was guzzling
muscatel.
The little maestro, *who*'d always had a thing for
her, hauled her out of the gutter and got her
vibrato back in gear.
The barber *who* found the nose in his croissant
never did get along with his wife.
The lamia, *who*'d entered the contest on a whim,
didn't sweat like the other girls.

(Actually a mythological beast, the lamia is passing herself off as a human teenager here, human pronoun and
all.)

Which refers only to animals and inanimate, unmoving
things. *That* refers to animals and things, and sometimes
to persons.

She tickled his fancy, *which* was in need of a
good laugh.

The lamia, which was a serpent
with human passions, is caught
here behind the scenes of her
inhuman powers.

The ocelot *that* she lost was wearing a costly fur
  coat.
The lamia, *which* was captured in a poem by
  Keats, was a serpent with human passions.

(Being once again an honest beast, the lamia wears the
pronoun appropriate to her species.)

Ask your crystal ball, *which* is the source and
  satiety of your prejudice.
This note, *which* she mangled in her pocket, lost
  its meaning in this fashion and place.
The chair *that* she chanced to sit in was wearing
  two pairs of boots.
An inamorata *that* oscillates can be exasperating.

What is an indefinite relative pronoun, which means that
it stands in for an undefined or unidentified antecedent
— like this:

I don't care *what* people say, my heart is not a
  piece of rock.
I know *what* I like, and I want it!
Take *what* you want and keep the change.
Think *what* you wish, I'm making my rounds on
  the wing.

To express a possessive relative pronoun, use either *whose*
or the forms *of whom* or *of which*.

The werewolf, *whose* fang I told you about, is in
  unbearable pain.
The werewolf, the wife *of whom* I mentioned,
  sobbed relentlessly.
We like werewolves *whose* teeth are in tip-top
  shape.

They prefer those chairs, the feet *of which* don't shuffle.

Compound relative pronouns are produced by adding *-ever* to *who, whom, what,* or *which.* These pronouns refer to any person or thing, without limit.

> Abandon yourself to *whatever* tickles your fancy.
> Nuzzle *whomever* you please.
> Ogle *whoever* pleases you.

Demonstrative Pronouns

Demonstrative pronouns point out. *This, that, these,* and *those* are demonstrative, pointing to whatever you want them to.

> *This* is my life
> *Those* are your desires.
> *These* are my misgivings.
> *That* is my answer.
> *This* is the procedure.
> *That's* what you think
> *Those* are insubordinate words.
> *These* are my knuckles.

Reciprocal Pronouns

Reciprocal pronouns *each other* and *one another* involve an exchange, however trite or bizarre.

The two maids cleaned *each other*.

The vampires gossiped with *one another* until the first gleam of morning light made them kiss *one another* good night.

The fauns were visibly fond of *each other* and polished *each other*'s hooves.

Reflexive and Intensive Pronouns

The reflexive and intensive are: *myself, yourself, herself, himself, itself, ourselves, yourselves,* and *themselves.* The same set fulfills both purposes, which we shall witness one at a time.

When used as reflexive pronouns, these function as objects or subjective complements. In other words, the subject and object are the same person, creature, or thing. As intensive pronouns, these same words are appositives.

The lamia gussied *herself* up (reflexive)

She held forth with *herself* about the relative merits of taffeta and crêpe de Chine. (reflexive)

Leopold *himself* is responsible for the loss of his bloomers. (intensive)

Reflexive Pronouns:

The vampire bit *himself*. (object)

The lamia admired *herself* in her beguiling new disguise. (object)

Yolanta put *herself* on guard. (object)

She made a pact with *herself* to never consort with fascists, pimps, or thugs. (object)

Hey, you just split an infinitive.

Alyosha was not *herself* today: she was rubbing
me with just her thumbs and staring off into
space. (subjective complement)

Keep these confidences to *yourself* and keep on
looking incredulous.
We have these snapshots of pink legs and
striped awnings to remind *ourselves* of our
vacation.
We have these snapshots of *ourselves* with pink
legs and striped awnings to recall our summer
vacation.

Intensive Pronouns

Intensive pronouns are *-self* pronouns you drag or invite
in for emphasis.

You *yourself* were casting a silhouette on the
shade.
I *myself* am the author of this spine-tingling
deed.
We *ourselves* often sleep in this schloss and leave
our ringlets and gauntlets in the covers.

The Self: Cautionary Tales

Don't use a *-self* pronoun where a personal pronoun belongs. It's tempting to do so when you're uncertain about
which case of the pronoun is called for: *I* or *me*? *Him* or
he? We'll puzzle over this shortly and briefly.

The self will come into your life with false credentials
and clutches of flowers — promising you the world, insin-

uating there's nothing it cannot do, nowhere it cannot go. Beware of this con artist who's stalked through history bamboozling impressionable minds and producing grammatical gaffes that have stained the honor of humble and noble families alike. The truth is, this interloper has its limits, and you should be on guard lest a *-self* pronoun come bounding in to knock off a rightful personal pronoun in its own territory.

Not:
Loona and *myself* always arrive late.
But:
Loona and *I* always arrive late.

Not:
Sophie and *himself* headed for the Dusty Cactus Saloon.
But:
Sophie and *he* headed for the Dusty Cactus.

Not:
Effie and *myself* are twin sisters.
But:
Effie and *I* are twin sisters.

Not:
Herself and Jean-Pierre shivered in the mist.
But:
She and Jean-Pierre shivered in the mist.

Expletive Pronouns

The expletive pronouns *it* and *there* come into our sentences as subjects when a clause or sentence lacks a plausible subject. For instance, the second clause in the preceding sentence could be written: "when there is no plausible subject of a clause or sentence." When the subject is a long clause, either of these two chameleons is a most accommodating sidekick to point the way through the subject and into the predicate more decisively. Then again, the expletive *it* or *there* is also summoned to emphasize a particular noun in the sentence.

> *There* is a house in New Orleans whose veranda is lined with satin.
> *There* are five more cupcakes than we have frosting for; I'll leave them for that loner by the river.
> *It*'s no use arguing with me; I've already made up all our minds.
> *It*'s your fault we lost the paddle.
> *There*'s no reason to get all hot and bothered over whether we're up the Danube or the Rhine.
> *It*'s a lonely soul who comes to jog in these woods.
> *It*'s chagrining to think that after we left they stayed up all night translating our witticisms and assertions into dog-eared Latin.

It's no use arguing with me; I've already made up all our minds.

Just In Case

When pronouns get together for a round of camaraderie and discipline, it's usually in cases. Cases determine their behavior in a given sentence—and sentences sentence them to certain cases, known as nominative, objective, and possessive. Word-weary as you are by now, you can guess what these must mean to the pronouns encased in them.

	Nominative Case	Objective Case	Possessive Case
Singular	I	me	my, mine
	she, he, it	her, him, it	her, hers, his, its
Plural	we	us	our, ours
	they	them	their, theirs
Singular & Plural	you	you	your, yours
	who	whom	whose

Only personal pronouns and the relative pronoun *who* change inflection for all three cases. Nouns in English, you've maybe noticed, don't change form when they slip into the objective case.

Nominative Case:

Nominative pronouns are subject pronouns; they include *I, you, he, she, it we, who, what, which,* and many more.

A subject pronoun functions either as the subject of a verb or as a subjective complement (you remember subjective complements, don't you?).

Subject of a Verb:

> *I* apologize.
> *He* forgives.

That feels marvelous.
This is even better.

Who complains?
Which of us is hurt?

I have always carried a fire in my heart for men
with hoofs in their loafers.

You're a southern Slav?
We're from Montenegro.

They ate their words in silence.

Subjective Complement:
The subjective complement always follows some form of
to be. Pronouns that insist on behaving in this fashion are
called predicate pronouns.

It is *she* who is dressed to kill.
It is *he* who was dragged in by the cat.
It is *I* who have hot pants.
The last one out of the burning bush was *he*.

Objective Case:
Pronouns in the objective case are called object pronouns, not objectionable. Object pronouns include *me*,
you, him, her, it, us, them, whom, which, this, that, these,
and *those*. As you see here, an object pronoun functions
as a direct object, an object of a preposition, an indirect
object, or the subject of an infinitive.

He likes *me*. (direct object)
He ordered taffeta rompers for *me*. (object of
preposition)
He sent *me* bonbons and hyacinths. (indirect
object)

He wants *me* to wash his odious socks. (subject of infinitive)

Direct Object:

I kissed *him*.

Whom did I desire?

He clasped *me*.

I ravished *it*.

Did you forget *these*?

They hustled *us*.

What makes you think I could possibly covet *that*?

Object of a Preposition:

Give a morsel of hope to *me*.

Go sing your succulent syllables to *him*.

Get that trashy trinket for *her*.

Give a morsel of hope to me.

They want to go to the anguished aquarium
    with *us*.
I like to hang around *them* on my weekends at
    the schloss.

Indirect Object:

Don't tell *me* you've been out with the boys!
She gave *him* the cold shoulder because they had
    a marmoreal love.
They sent *us* a bill for damages to the canopies
    and crocus beds.
He gave *her* a recording of Mahler's *Tenth*
    because he was not quite finished with her.

Subject of an Infinitive:

She wanted *him* to slumber in her wake.
He wished *her* to tuck him in first.

Possessive Case:

The possessive case is used to denote ownership or to
attribute a quality or characteristic to someone or something. A pronoun in the possessive case may stand in for
that someone or something, as the following examples of
possessive personal pronouns demonstrate:

My thoughts are guarded by indiscretion.
Thank you for *your* inscrutable honesty.
It took the prince a while to find *her* lips.
We put *our* best feet forward and crushed each
    other's toes.
Their samovar was stolen, along with all *their* left
    socks and shoes.
They trampled on *my* nightie, those
    shortsighted mastodons.
Our mozzarella comes from the most contented
    or contentious buffaloes.

To form the possessive case of an indefinite pronoun, just add the apostrophe and an *s* to the pronoun.

> *someone's* misfortune
> *anyone's* boo-boo
> *everyone's* fault
> *no one's* misdemeanor

> He likes to consider *anything's* qualities and then exalt them into *someone's* sorrow.

For personal pronouns, there is *no* apostrophe in the possessive case.

> The weltschmerz is *his.*
> The ennui is *hers.*
> That slab of marble is *ours.*
> These footnotes in the sand are *theirs.*

The relative or interrogative pronoun in the possessive case is also quite complete without an apostrophe.

> *Whose* is this libretto?
> The maestro, *whose* lips were quivering, was about to make himself scarce.

Possessive pronouns are often used with gerunds.

> We admired *her* curtseying.
> She resented *our* clapping.
> *Their* flashing about has a purpose not apparent to their aunties in town.
> *Their* rousing hostilities among the Bosoxians could mean a long, embittered wait for coffee and soap.

Were you clapping your tails against the rocks?

In Case You Were Wondering

In sentences with a compound joined by *and* or *or*, use the same case — nominative or objective — as you would with no compound.

My frothing steed and I are on the make.

(We arrive at this case choice by letting the steed foam his way out of the sentence altogether so that only the *I* remains: *I* am on the make. Don't let the verb change throw you: it's the pronoun with which you are so intrigued.)

Let's see how this works with two pronouns:

> Him and me cracked crawdads.
> *check-up:*
> Him cracked crawdads. Me cracked crawdads, too!
> *He* cracked crawdads. *I* did, too.
> *He* and *I* cracked crawdads.

> Lucifer shot a dirty look at she and I.
> Lucifer shot a dirty look at she. He gave I a pretty nasty once-over as well.
> Lucifer shot a dirty look at *her*. Then he only had eyes for *me*.
> Lucifer shot a dirty look at *her* and *me*.

> This summons is from Sir Gallimauf and I.
> Well? This summons is from *me*.
> So it's: This summons is from Sir Gallimauf and *me*.

(You know better than to say "from I," so just knock Sir Gallimauf out of the way for a moment and try on those pronouns without him.)

A pronoun with a noun appositive after it goes by the same case as it would without the noun.

> Us mastodons need space.
> Us need space? *We* need space.
> *We* mastodons need space.
>
> They brought the marzipan for *us* mastodons,
>   with the intention of keeping us quiet.
> *We* otherworldly creatures must stick together.

Similar fidelity holds where a pronoun appositive appears: it still takes the same case as the word to which it's in apposition.

> Keeping late hours keeps them — Dafne and *him*
>   — in touch with paranormal occurrences.
>
> Let's you and *me* stick together from now on.
> Let's you and *me* get together and do away with
>   some of the possibilities. (*you* and *me* are in
>   apposition to the *us* in let's: let us)

A pronoun, in an incomplete comparison, has the same case as it would if the comparison were complete.

> You're considerably more sanguine about these
>   threats than *I*. (than I am)
> Blaze Cinders is not nearly as magnetic or free-
>   spirited as *she*. (as she is)
> Any faun or stevedore would easily be more
>   gallant then *he*. (than he is)

Let's you and me get together and do away with some of the possibilities.

Who and Whom

When we come to *who* and *whom*, presence of mind might help. What's tricky is keeping track of subjects and objects, direct and indirect, while keeping an eye on the convolutions among the clauses they're caught in. It's worth a shot just trying to stare them down. If that's not enough, leap your way through this book to the "Clauses" chapter, where you will acquire wisdom, understanding, and a new perspective or hair color to accompany you back to this page.

> We must warn *whomever* we meet about the rat
>   pack on a spree.
> We warned *whoever* came our way about the
>   small but agile danger.

In the first warning, there's really no question: the warned one or ones is twice an object: both met and warned. In the second, the warned one is a subject in its own clause (yes, do go spend some time with those "Clauses") and therefore has a right to the nominative case — i.e., who(ever).

> *Who* else might happen along to be taken into
>   the matter at hand?
> *Whom* else might we come across to kidnap into
>   this game?

> He let out a low whistle, bit his lip, and tossed
>   the note to his cousin, *whom* he noticed
>   floating by on a barge.

Turn it around, make it a statement:

> He noticed *she* or *her*?
> He noticed her. (her = whom; she = who)

> This is my brother, *whom* I've been expecting to
>   arrive for days.
> I've been expecting *him* to arrive.
> This is my brother, *who* I told you is
>   inordinately fond of jails.

I told you *he* is fond. You were told, and are therefore
the object; he is the subject of a subordinate clause.

> Errata is the nymph *who* I think is Effie's twin.
> Effie is the nymph *who* has taken the flash out of
>   his hoofs.

> You're the one in *whom* I can confide.
>   How did I arrive at that?
>   I can confide in *her*.
> You're the only one *who*'ll listen!

> Leopold is the one *who* I believe lost his
>   bloomers.

> Frisk *whoever* enters. Frisk *whomever* you
>   suspect.
> Show the door to *whoever* resists.

> Invite *whoever* is gullible enough to come.

> Give the lagniappe to *whoever* comes first.

> Apologize to *whomever* you've miffed.

And whom are *you*?

I suspect that some of the who/whom confusion comes
with placement. When one of them is supposed to begin
a sentence, it tricks you into thinking it's the subject, and
so, of course, it must be *who:*

> Who else would I expect to run into on a dark
> staircase at this hour?

Does that sound vaguely right? It doesn't sound jarring-
ly wrong — at least, perhaps? But this familiar menace,
whoever he/she is, is *not* the subject, but is, as those
whom we were warning, above, the object: I would expect to run into him/her. And I would expect him/her.
But to run is what's being expected, and whom/him/her
is thus likely to be run into. So it's:

> *Whom* else would I expect to run into on a dark
> staircase at this hour?

Demotically speaking, we take our liberties. How often
do you expect to hear "Whom do you think you're kid-
ding?"? Here again, it's the first word in the sentence —
isn't that enough to give it at least a quasi-subject status?
But *whom* is (or is not) being kidded, and is the object
(however wide of the mark) whom someone is rhetori-
cally failing to fool. Still, with all those boggled attempts,
we begrudge the subject its total dominion over the
nominative case. And maybe if someone's being kidded,
or not, he/she has in the process acquired immunity to
the prescribed case — and can go on to the next chal-
lenge: Who(m) do you think you are, anyway?

❧ Agreements ❧

We know what's going on in a sentence, what the subject and predicate are up to, partly through how parts of speech agree with one another: verb forms matching the subject's state and shenanigans, pronouns aping their antecedents. Often these issues are so easy and apparent that you scarcely bat an eye. More dubious situations arise quite frequently, however, and in this chapter we'll stare down these complexities till they cease to baffle us.

A verb, for instance, agrees with its subject in number, despite any distractions from just what that number is. Verbs need to agree in person as well as number. The first person is speaking (as I am here); the second is being spoken to, and may be listening; the third person is being spoken about. At this moment, the third person is the sentence. The number, where agreements are concerned, is either singular or plural. Collective nouns get into the act here with their own confusions, as do some of the less common plural forms, including words that feel at once both singular and plural. A pronoun, too, will aptly reflect the number of its antecedent: *they* does not refer to one person, no matter how many personalities she or he has, or how eager you are to skirt the gender frays.

Subject-Verb Agreement (with some pronouns tagging along)

Intervening words between subject and verb don't have to ruffle a sentence's intent. A phrase inhabiting the ground between them is no cause for the subject and verb to disagree. The same is true for a pronoun that's within shouting distance of its antecedent.

> An *entourage* of hangers-on *was* sprawling in the lounge.
>
> One *thing* after another *has* thrown the troll off-kilter.
>
> An *abundance* of rumpled dahlias *was* deposited at death's door.
>
> The *lingua franca* in these parts *is* Rumanian mixed with blood and cash.
>
> The *afternoon* of the fauns *flies* past in a flash of hoofs.
>
> This *house* with its skeletons in the closets *is* all there is to my abode.

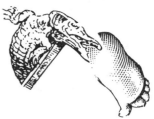

> An *assortment* of odd chocolates and soft toffees *was* congealed in her alligator shoes.
>
> This *resurgence* of ethnic tensions *comes* as no surprise to Timofey.
>
> The *bat* suspended from Loona's hairdo *was* repulsed by her Nuit Blanche perfume.
>
> A *coven* of baby witches and warlocks *has* been moving in next door.

A *family* of Celtic werewolves *was* off for a
  picnic on the moor.

A clause coming between the subject and the verb
doesn't affect their covenant, either. We are so accustomed to a sibilant sound signaling a plural verb that we
are often fooled.

The *nymph* who left these footprints *is* usually
  much more cautious.
The *way* you're wearing those pajamas *is* bound
  to give the sandman pause.
The *robot* you've been sending flowers to *is*
  wearing his heart on his sleeve.

Here, there are agreements of both sorts:

The *robot* . . . is wearing *his* heart on *his* sleeve.

The number of the subject isn't fazed by parenthetical
expressions introduced by such words as *like*, *with*, *no less
than*, *together with*, *as well as*, or *including*.

Her *smile*, with its intimations of unspeakable
  pleasures, *has* been of little use of late.
His *affability*, no less than his dashing good
  looks, *makes* him a wanted man in this town.
The *tower*, including all its grotesque
  inhabitants, *is* going on tour in the spring.
Rosie, together with the cabbie, *is* rounding the
  corner in a cab.
The *juggernauts*, as well as their chaperon, *have*
  tendered their thanks to the host.
You, like I, *are* to emerge from the fracas
  unscathed.
Weltschmerz, in addition to ennui, *gives* our
  courtship a real flair.

Do Alyosha and Jean-Pierre
ever get away from
that church?

Even when a subject comes hot on the heels of its verb,
it is still the verb that must agree in number with the
subject.

> *Are* the sandman and the vampire buddies?
> *Do* Alyosha and Jean-Pierre ever get away from
> that church?
> *Have* that gargoyle and his girlfriend accepted
> an invitation to Smolensk?

Exceptions:

If the two subjects refer to the same person or thing, the verb is singular.

> My sidekick and bête noire *has* arrived.

(*Sidekick* and *bête noire* identify the same difficult companion.)

> Campari and soda *is* the little maestro's usual libation.
> That surly bloke and bounder *is* a bona fide M.P.
> Gabor's colleague and compatriot *plays* a mean alto sax.

My sidekick and bête noire has arrived.

My coiffeur and confidant *says* he can't take any more of my tangled hair and tales.

Another exception turns up when *each* or *every* precedes singular subjects joined by *and*; then again a singular verb will do the trick.

> Each huzzah and hallelujah *was* bouncing off the dome.
> Every truncheon and hatchet *was* safely in its place.

Two or more singular subjects joined by *or* or *nor* waltz to the same singular verb.

> The nymph or the lamia *was* twining her legs around this tree.
> The robot or the dentist *has* requested a tango of Gardel's.
> Neither the gargoyle nor the chimera *has* hidden veins of gold.
> Effie or Errata *is* tossing her garland over the sleeping faun's horns.
> Neither the dancer nor the dance *has* bared the music's soul.

When singular and plural subjects are joined by the correlative conjunctions *either . . . or, neither . . . nor, not only . . . but also, not . . . but,* the verb begs to agree with the subject nearest to it.

> Neither kitsch nor its *proponents were* ridiculed out of the show.
> Not only the patrons but also the *curator was* unduly cruel.
> Neither nuclear war nor meteor *showers have* hurt the dahlia crop this year.

Not the vampires but the *sandman has* made a
mess of this schloss.

Neither Jean-Pierre nor Pauline and her *sisters
have* ever guzzled such a storm.

Not the maestro but his *sycophants have* decided
to blow this joint.

Neither yellow roses nor an X-rated *nosegay is*
going to lure this marriage off the rocks.

Where a singular subject and a plural one are together
in the same sentence with this kind of affirmative/nega-
tive construction, the verb agrees in number with the
affirmative subject, which makes a lot more sense if you
take a good look at these sentences:

All the gargoyles but not a single man *were*
obliging to her.

The werewolf and not the vampires *has* done me
injury.

The vampires and not the werewolf *have*
harmed me bodily.

Neither Jean-Pierre nor
Pauline and her sisters have
ever guzzled such a storm.

It is with its subject that a verb agrees, not with its subjective complement.

His pantaloons *are* a problem for the king.
The king's problem *is* his pantaloons.

Her hankerings *are* her downfall.
Her downfall *is* her hankerings.

Vertices *are* the ecstasy of triangles.
The ecstasy of triangles *is* vertices.

Those *spats are* not the real reason you've been
summoned by Sir Gallimauf.

Narcotics is one of several
shady businesses that the
government indulges.

Nouns that are plural in form but singular in meaning
and use take singular verbs. Among these nouns we find
physics, ethics, mathematics, dominoes (the game and not its
pieces), *checkers, news, mumps, measles, molasses, summons,*

customs (that deals with borders and trafficking), *narcotics*, *economics*, *statistics* (when you are referring to the study, not specific figures), *politics*, and *acrobatics*.

> *Politics is* the passion of the very cruel and the
>   very just.
> *Mumps is* deforming the vampires.
> *Ethics is* her toughest subject.
> *Narcotics is* one of several shady businesses that
>   the government indulges.
> The *summons is* from Sir Gallimauf.
> The *molasses* in the gingerbread *is* overwhelming
>   the mastodons.
> *Astrophysics is* Guillaume's usual profession, but
>   his performance in *Four Nights of a Dreamer*
>   revealed a sultry beauty and grace of body on
>   the prowl in an earthly orbit.
> *Customs doesn't* mind if our satchels are loaded
>   with grief.

Headquarters takes a singular or plural verb. The plural usually applies to place:

> The rats' *headquarters are* in Amsterdam.
> Their *headquarters were* raided in connection
>   with a missing Stilton.

But the singular verb is more apt when authority, not physical location, is designated by the word:

> *Headquarters gives* its go-ahead now that the
>   ramekins have been distributed.

The shade of sadness we call the blues can take a singular or plural verb, since anyone who has them can't be bothered to look it up, or to be consistent about whether it is — or they are — in pieces or in a solid hopeless mass.

The *blues is* hard to lose.
The *blues have* tracked me down in this upbeat
    part of town.

Some nouns name things that have two moving parts joined together. Many of these, with their plural forms but singular intentions, take plural verbs: *scissors, pliers, tweezers*; and, no matter who is wearing them, *handcuffs, trousers,* and *tights.*

My tights *are* in my locker, with my diaphragm.
The pliers *were* used to open her mouth, which
    was refusing to speak.
The scissors had made a mess of the heavens'
    geometry and *were* preparing to swoop down
    on Earth.
Her trousers *were* held up by a pair of
    suspenders that clutched her waist with tiny
    hands.

Pronoun-Verb Agreement

Singular pronouns take singular verbs. And what might these pronouns be? And must you go riffling off, losing your place here and forgetting what you're after and ending up in a field of cows? To hold your gaze, I'll tell you this much: they include (these pronouns): *each, either, neither, everybody, everyone, anybody, anyone, somebody, someone, nobody,* and *no one.*

Everyone is waltzing to a different Johann
    Strauss.
Neither of them *was* eager for the contretemps
    to end.

"*Someone's* been sleeping in my bed," cried the baby vampire, snuffling at his dank cradle of earth. (Someone *has:* vampires start making contractions with their very first words.)

Neither of those juggernauts *is* on the guest list for the next two seasons.

This treatment also goes for expressions like *and his uncle* (in the following sentence), which is really part of *every-*

Neither of them was eager for the contretemps to end.

Everyone and his uncle is
studying podiatry.

one, since *everyone* embraces, with utter abandon, each
and every leaf and twig, bud and bug, on every family
tree.

Everyone and his uncle *is* studying podiatry.

The uncle is a deliberate redundancy to emphasize how
widely this study is taking hold.

Any, all, such, and *none* may be singular or plural, depending on how you are sizing up the situation or are
attempting to put words into another's mouth. The an-
swer you hope or expect to elicit, your grasp of the particulars and how lasting their union will be — these are

but a few of the matters you might ponder as you choose your verb forms and make history, sway minds, and cast lots.

> *Is any* of you fine fauns or fellows available for a folie à deux?
> *Are any* of you guys with the shaggy shoes interested in a run around the lake?
> *Have any* of you made up your minds?
> *Do all* of your heads need scratching?
> *Are all* of us going to be punished?
> *Is all* the cake devoured?
> *Are all* the pastries so prepossessing?
> *Are such undulations* part of your everyday gestural vocabulary?
> *Is such* a humid *snout* something that runs in your family?

Collective Nouns

Collective nouns can be confusing when you're conjugating their verbs and giving them possessions: When is *this* word an *it*, and at what point does *they* take over? The catch-all term we know them by does not hint at how the lines blur when a writer contemplates a crowd. This contemplation will usually involve your quantifying the will within this collection and deciding whether its parts or members are all acting together or with several minds and motions.

Before we move on to the herd of bulls in the china shop, we'll deal with the simpler kind of collective noun that refers to a class of things always taken together. These nouns never multiply into plurality: they remain singular when it comes to the verbs and pronouns that help place them in your thoughts and writing. These include *luggage*, *baggage*, *cutlery*, and *equipment*. Another way to put the quirk that distinguishes them from the herd of collective nouns awaiting us is this: never will you have occasion to write *luggages*, *baggages*, *cutleries*, or *equipments*.

> My *luggage has* been missing since we landed in Smolensk.
> His *equipment is* lousy, but *it's* being replaced.
> Mind the *cutlery*; *it's* sharper than you think.

(Note that these nouns take singular pronouns as well as verbs.)

As for the other collective nouns, we've been playing with them all along. The first sentences in this chapter spun us through a zoetropic tour of such words: the sprawling entourage, the abundance of dahlias, the assortment of bonbons, the household of precocious necromancers, and a family long in the tooth. In each of those sentences, the members of the group were acting together, and demonstrating the rule that collective nouns should go through their motions with singular verbs when the collection is behaving as a unit. And when it calls on a pronoun to step into its many, many shoes, a singular pronoun will oblige. As we'll see, though, very soon, there may be times when you want to imply more willfulness within the ranks, to split some hairs, or to send things packing in several directions at once. Be of several minds about it, then, and let that ambivalence show. You don't always get to take such liberties with crowds.

> A whole *welter* of enthusiasms *isn't* enough to get this thing off the ground.

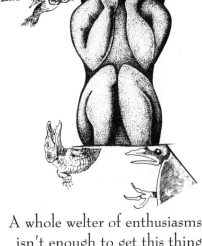

A whole welter of enthusiasms isn't enough to get this thing off the ground.

The *pantheon disapproves.*

The *coven is* gathering and cavorting on the
   shore.

The *congregation is* rising in fervent harmony to
   sing Handel's "My Heart Is Throbbing."

The *caravan is* pausing for iced tea and sherbet
   at the Now You See It Now You Don't
   Caravanserai Café. (Hunger and thirst, if
   nothing else, will induce man and beast to act
   at times in unison.)

The *coven has* voted to move *its* sabbath to a
   grove of olive trees.

The *grove was* not consulted about this, nor have
   its wishes ever been considered since the days
   when the gods showed their faces among *its*
   shadows.

The *quintet is* acting in concert on this move to
   hijack the plane.

Collective nouns take plural verbs when the group is
meant to be thought of as individuals.

The *committee were* shuffling *their* feet and
   scratching *their* many heads.

As the fire blazed, the *octet were* rushed to the
   open door, but only two escaped.

Is there a sacred *set* of unspoken rules that
   mollifies our rages into self-righteous zeal?

Here, if you want to imply that each individual rule mollifies the rages (as well as make those rules' combined
effect more powerful), you could write it like this:

Is there a sacred set of unspoken rules that
   mollify our rages into self-righteous zeal?

The first way gives the impression that it is only in their joining forces that these rules can bring about moral intolerance. Often, the best reference to consult is your own vision. What's the picture you see when naming a group and stirring it to action? Do its individual parts retain their identities, or does the collection so thoroughly engulf them that *they* no longer exist?

In writing "A *number* of sleeves *dangle* from the coat and *break* into urgent gestures," I didn't consult a range *or* a clump of authorities to tell me what's going on in that closet. I stuck my head in and saw for myself that each sleeve had its own emotions and story, so the verb had to express this plurality of commotion.

Following are some other vignettes where such images play out these thoughts.

Those rats! How do *they* sort out these verb-and-pronoun conundrums while carrying on their business as a gang?

> The *rat pack keeps its* gun loaded at all times.
> The *rat pack* all *have* whiskers of different
>   lengths and textures, and individual bank
>   accounts.

And here's another group living and breathing as one, until it becomes too much to bear:

> The *ménage à trois is* rousing *itself* or trundling
>   off to sleep.
> The *ménage à trois are* going back on *their* vows
>   and *are* going *their* separate ways.

When *couple* and *pair* refer to people, they usually treat themselves to plurals.

The bright young *couple* who'*ve* moved into the
neighborhood *seem* oblivious to the perils that
threaten their Wisconsin cheddars and
Danish blues.

As we have already noted, collective nouns may take a
singular or plural pronoun, depending on their meanings.

The entourage is abandoning *its* turf and is
walking out in a huff. (It was moving as a
unit.)
The entourage lolling about in the lobby were
hanging out *their* tongues. (Apparently this
was an existential act for each of them.)

The ménage à trois is rousing
itself or trundling itself
off to sleep.

The Styrian String Quartet is a four-headed
 monster of catgut and mediocrity that
 shouldn't be let out of *its* cage.
The vampire *family* have been shuffling *their*
 coffins around and confusing *their* domiciles.

When taken as a unit (most often gladly), sums of money
and measurements go with a singular verb.

Twenty years *is* the maximum I am willing to
 suffer this ruckus with you.
Forty francs *is* too much for this woebegone
 Mimolette.
Five hundred bucks *is* not much bail for a
 recalcitrant debutante.

When the sum of money or measurement doesn't so
neatly present itself as a unit, it finds a plural verb to get
lost with.

These five hundred dog-eared dollars all *bear*
 portraits of a borzoi named Borian in the face
 of George Washington.
The twenty years that just flew past *have* not
 taken their leave of my youth.

A literary, dramatic, or musical title takes a singular verb,
even if it contains a plural subject. The same goes for the
name of an artwork, a dance piece, or a film.

"Tidings from Timofey," a Slavic ghost story,
 concerns a specter who is afraid of the dark.
Gabor said that *The Enigma Variations is* a piece
 of claptrap scored for ruffians in chintz.
Ruffians in Chintz is being greeted with hoopla
 and catcalls from the West End to East
 Berlin.

But it was *written* for *me*.

The Brothers Karamazov is missing from my shelf.

Sunny Smith's inspired *Legal Briefs does* indeed have lawyers dancing in their underwear, with their briefcases, and a pair of judges sexual-harassingly cohabiting a single pompous robe.

Fear and Trembling in the Aquarium is a cantata about angst in the lower forms of life.

The Frogs is not a Greek tragedy about a bewitchment in a scummy pond.

"Fear and Trembling in the Aquarium" is a cantata about angst in the lower forms of life.

Words considered as words are always singular, too, and
thus take singular verbs.

> *Lycanthropes is* the more scientific name for
>   werewolves.
> *Antipodes means* places diametrically opposite on
>   our sphere, and *extends its* embrace to include
>   earthly inhabitants so related.

Plural forms of nouns like *automaton, criterion,* and *phe-
nomenon* end in *-a* and jump, quite naturally, only when
plural verbs call to them. Other examples of these
Graeco-Roman survivors include *bacteria, errata,* and
strata.

> Among the *phenomena* that *interest* her *are*
>   butterflies, fireflies, and flying frogs.
> The *automata were* choosing their dance
>   partners while a soufflé exploded in the
>   cloakroom.

Data and *media* are plurals formed in the same way, but
over time have come to take singular as well as plural
verbs, with the distinctions occasionally blurring to no
one's mortification. *Data* is usually a plural noun meaning facts or pieces of information ("The data add up to a
picture of . . ."). As a singular mass noun, it's given a
singular treatment ("Not much data has been raked up
on . . ."). *Media* has developed into a collective noun,
often with singular verb, but as with other collective
nouns, the choice will depend on the situation, the particular picture:

> The data, *say* the media, *do* not suggest any
>   back-room tinkering with the mannequins'
>   toes.

The media's been coming down hard on
    podiatry lately, which has only brought more
    business and increased enrollment in podiatry
    schools.

In sentences that begin with the expletive *there* (as in
there is, there are, there exists, there exist), the subject follows the verb and has the last word about whether that
verb is singular or plural. *There* is not the subject, nor
will it ever be.

    Not:
There *exists* many beasts in the wilderness that I'd rather
not discuss.
    But:
There *exist* many beasts in the wilderness that I'd rather
not discuss.

    There *is* one lonely mummy in the tomb.
    There *are* cronies one is better off without.

    There *is* a faun in the forest who looks like
        Blaise Cendrars.
    There *are* wraiths among the pachyderms who
        prefer to go unnamed.

That *there* is not the same use and meaning as the adverb
there that's saying "in that place."

    There she sobbed.
    There he placed his paw.
    There you go again.
    There's my runaway son!

There's my runaway son!

As with the expletive *there*, when a construction opens with *here is* or *here are*, the number of the verb should fit the subject, which will appear after the verb.

> Here *is* my time sheet.
> Here *are* the horseshoes.
> Here's a little something for your trouble.
> Here *are* the dreaded dahlias.

The expletive *it* wouldn't know what to do with a plural verb. Give it what it knows and loves, and not an identity crisis.

> It *is* the little maestro and his hangers-on.
> It *was* the vampires who paid a visit to the schloss.
> It *is* that ingenue who has such panache.
> It *is* wolves that are known as the Children of the Night.

Pronouns, or
Pronoun-Antecedent Agreement

Pronouns and their antecedents are made for each other. An *antecedent* itself is rarely on its own: there'll always be a possessive pronoun nearby, watching anxiously, flashing the wedding ring. In order for this relationship to last through a single sentence, however, they have to meet halfway, agreeing in number at the very least, never mind about the intimate details that every such coupling brings to your writing. Singular pronouns, then, will rush in to join such antecedents as *person, man, woman, someone, somebody, anyone, anybody, either, neither, each, everyone,* and *everybody.*

Personally I can't imagine anyone but the most per-
verted grammarian calling anything an antecedent for
long, which *anything* would be here right now if we could
just get *it* paired up with—there, that's done, we can
leave *them* together now. (And there's another one.)

> *Everyone* scratched *his* own forearm and took
> another drag.
> *Each* of the suppliants was given *his* or *her* own
> licorice whip.

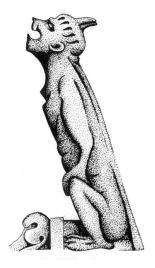

If you prefer, for reasons of gallantry, feminism, or fidelity to the sequence of this distribution, that *her* precede
his, try saying "her or his," and if you and your readers
enjoy gargling in the middle of a sentence, then by all
means do so, or even sign up for lessons with Pauline
and Jean-Pierre.

The ubiquitous *their* is always waiting to snatch up
any unattached antecedents and toss them into its collection (harem?). As a pronoun on the make, it's enjoyed a
smashing success—especially in spoken language. Here,
as in so many matters of agreement, it's your discretion,
your sense of it all, that will finally decide how to hand
out your possessions and possessives, your *him*s, *her*s, and
*them*s. One way out is to rewrite a sentence so you avoid
the dilemma altogether. For instance, in the above licorice handout, you could shift the passive voice from the
whips to their recipients: "Licorice whips were handed
out to everyone." *Or* you could say, simply, "Everyone
got a licorice whip." But it's not quite the same, is it?
The focus and emphasis alight elsewhere with each sub-
tle move or removal. To me, "Everyone's coloring their
hair these days" sounds fine, even though it's inconsis-
tent—with first a singular verb and then a plural possessive for the same "everyone." Gradually, a contradiction
like this comes to sound familiar, the Procrusteans and

pundits grumble, then nod off, and no one *is* left who *cares*. But if you waffle around in this area, don't always keep a straight face. One knowing look or wink could bring a lost, lonely, or divorced antecedent caterwauling from across a crowded room.

> *We* have aces up *our* sleeves.
> *I*'d give *my* eyeteeth to know how come *you*'re
>   wearing *your* mouth at such a jaunty angle.
> Jean-Pierre and I got *our* passports.
> *Anyone* who's ready to do *her* number should
>   stand behind the cello.
> The robot and the dentist showed *their* smooth
>   and hairy legs.
> I like hanging out with lycanthropes because *it*
>   makes me feel like one of the boys.

(The antecedent of *it* is the gerund phrase "hanging out with lycanthropes," a singular thing to like.)

> If *someone* has a complaint, *she/he gets* to bellow
>   it in the public square.

Waffling and waffled version:

> If *someone* has a complaint, *they get* to bellow it
>   in the public square.

Whether relative pronouns (*who, which, that, what*) are singular or plural depends on their antecedents, still calling the shots.

> He's the only chaperon *who has* been so easy to
>   lose.
> He is one of many chaperons *who have* tangled
>   with the juggernauts.

Those mastodons *who wear* braces are having
trouble with the marzipan.

(Yes, I know *who* refers to people, but I'm anthropomor-
phizing these beasts or bestializing those fellows.)

It is I *who am* the culprit in "The Case of the
Missing Gorgonzola."

Two or more antecedents joined by *and* take a plural
pronoun.

Samson and Delilah licked *their* chops.
Rosie and Nimrod rubbed *their* flanks.
Alyosha and Jean-Pierre have lost *their* luggage.

Singular antecedents joined by *or* or *nor* take a pronoun
that's also singular.

Neither Nimbus nor Quercus will present *his*
rosebud to the queen.

In reference to one singular and one plural antecedent,
the pronoun agrees with the nearer antecedent.

Neither abduction nor nuptials had *their* place
on the agenda for tonight.
Neither nuptials nor abduction had *its* place on
the agenda for tonight.

Demonstrative pronouns (*this, that, these, those*) prefer to
agree with the nouns they're seen with.

Not:
She has a propensity for *those* sort of muddles.
But:
➤ She has a propensity for *that* sort of muddle.
Or:
➤ She has a propensity for *those* sorts of muddles.

You're not the *kind* of girl who'd steal my
handkerchief.

That's not even the *kind* of handkerchief I'd give
to my pet rabbit.

What *sort* of rabbit would girls steal
handkerchiefs for?

What *sorts* of handkerchiefs have sent you to the
clink in the past?

These *kinds* of frailties are best left unexposed.

Those *kinds* of women are best left unespoused.

That's not the *sort* of bang we were supposed to
go out with.

❧ Phrases ❧

This chapter could be called "We've Been Here All Along." Without phrases, sentences would be starkly inhospitable or would lumber beneath the weight of adjectives and adverbs piled on so thickly that they'd bring no pictures to our minds. That's it: we'd be bored as listeners and talkers, readers and writers if we had only adjectives and adverbs to modify and describe actions, faces, and purpose. This is where phrases swoop in, lifting us up, knocking us over, shoving us aside, setting us down (all with prepositional phrases giving direction to their nouns and verbs)—or, as that series of participial phrases just did, they move us in space or emotion.

So nimbly and neatly tucked into other messages, a phrase can deceive you into slighting its significance. If I say,

> The rats in drag, on the lam, struggled
> with their luggage into the coach,

I'm giving or hinting at an enormous amount of information in these small, oh-by-the-way, throwaway words. The essential subject and predicate of the sentence amount to: "The rats struggled." But look at the drama going on in the four prepositional phrases! There a whole story unwinds: that the rats are fugitives (meaning someone's on to them), dressed in women's clothes (which they acquired, it seems, along the way — by theft, or barter, or exchange at gunpoint), and are taking their stuff with them in an antiquated vehicle (and where *that* came into the picture could be quite a story in itself).

Phrases can lighten the telling of any story, and stop you from hopping one staccato sentence to another up and down the page. (Phrases, too, can be overused, especially when a string of prepositional phrases could be reworded with more variety.) With a phrase, you are somehow several places at once, flicking and alighting amid all the particulars of subject, object, and verb, along that exhilarating edge where they meet. Herein lurks the danger of your modifying what you don't mean to; but for now, let's see what these phrases can do for us when they're not making mischief. In their endless combinations, phrases add rhythm — darting, gliding, tumbling, ambling, as well as putting things in their place.

Being able to recognize a group of words as a phrase — seeing it as a unit — helps you in writing, editing, and reading: in avoiding or repairing fragments and comma splices, in sorting out questions about agreements, and in moving, or otherwise setting to rights, dangling and misplaced modifiers.

A phrase, made up of several words, usually acts as a single word — most often an adjective or adverb, although occasionally (and controversially, on the Procrustean circuit) it can behave as a noun. Lacking a subject-predicate combination, a phrase can't do much of anything alone, but it's positively a virtuoso when it comes to embellishing, showing relationships, and giving you many different ways to arrange the rest of the sentence, which *it needs* to fulfill its promise.

The two most ubiquitous kinds of phrases are prepositional and verbal. Having knocked around with plenty of prepositions and verbals by now (and you're doing so in this sentence, if you needed any reminders), you'll probably be able to tell one from the other. Verbal phrases, of course, come in three types: infinitive, participial, and gerund. They're all bound to become more familiar by the time we catch up with the rats again toward the end of this chapter.

Here, before we dawdle with each type and its virtuosity, are all of them. We've seen them before, under different lights.

Prepositional Phrase:

The afternoon *of the fauns* flies past *in a flash of hoofs*.

Infinitive Phrase:

The quintet is acting in concert on this move *to hijack the plane*.

Participial Phrase:

"Someone's been sleeping in my bed," cried the baby vampire, *snuffling at his dank cradle of earth*. (*of earth*, what do you know, is a prepositional phrase tagging along with the participial)

Gerund Phrase:

Bellowing complaints in the square at dawn left half the population with laryngitis and the remainder plagued with doubts.

Prepositional Phrases

A prepositional phrase is made up of a preposition and its co-conspirators — the object of the preposition and any modifiers that modify its own modifications (qualities rarely come alone, after all). With all this riffraff, though, the phrase itself still acts like a single part of speech: as an adjective, an adverb, or, more rarely, a noun.

The nude *in the next room* slid down the wall.
  (adjective)
The nude is *in the next room*. (adjective, as
  subjective complement)
The nude went *into the next room*. (adverb)
In the next room is where the nude holds court.
  (noun)

Adjective:

That gargoyle is *of unknown origin*.
This one is *from Prague*.
The damsel *with the bedroom eyes* is my grandma.
Her mug, *with its inscrutable torpor*, is
  enthralling.
The little maestro greeted an unexpected guest,
  a beast *to whom he was allergic*.
Do you know the way *out of here*?
The afternoon *of the faun* did not end in
  tragedy.
There is a midriff *beneath his paw*.
The sandman, *in cahoots with the vampire*, lays
  the subject to rest.
At odds with her sedentary companions, the
  wildebeest teamed up with the crestfallen
  lamia in a game *of Violer le Duc*.
I fancy dames *with broad shoulders*.

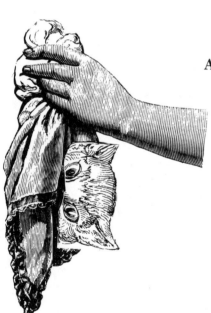

The little maestro greeted an
unexpected guest, a beast to
whom he was allergic.

I fancy dames with broad
shoulders.

Adverb:

> *With shoulders like those*, she can shrug off my
> problems as well as her own.
>
> He beat me *at a game* of hearts *in a field* of
> digitalis.
>
> The proselytizer hopped *over the threshold*.
>
> The housecoated heathen hissed raffishly
> *through her teeth*.
>
> At odds with her sedentary companions, the
> wildebeest teamed up *with the crestfallen lamia
> in a game* of Violer le Duc.

He tugged *on her tutu.*
An impresario was wolf-whistling *in the wings.*

Noun:

Out of my depth is where I'm likely to be.
Beyond the pale is the penultimate stop of this
   train.
Beneath the bridge is a fine place for befriending
   trolls.
Out to lunch is where he's been all week.

To nuzzle flagpoles is her
secret desire.

Verbal Phrases

Infinitive Phrases:
Bring together an infinitive and an object, and you have
an infinitive phrase to use as an all-purpose noun, an
adjective, or an adverb.

Noun:

To nuzzle flagpoles is her secret desire. (subject)
She longs *to nuzzle flagpoles.* (direct object)
Her secret longing is *to nuzzle flagpoles.*
   (subjective complement)
She has no purpose in life except *to nuzzle
   flagpoles.* (object of preposition *except*)
Sylvie loves *to split infinitives.* (direct object)
There is nothing I want of my lovers but *to
   loosen my mortal coils.* (object of preposition
   but)
Timofey has few more pressing desires in death
   than *to visit Bosnia.* (object of preposition *than*)

Adjective:

> I have a suggestion *to thrust upon you*. (modifies *suggestion*)
>
> That jar of marzipan cookies is *to put the mastodons at ease*. (modifies *jar*)
>
> Those are not windows *to undress in*. (modifies *windows*)
>
> Where are the blue highways *to slow down on?* (modifies *highways*)
>
> I have my gold feathers *to hang out with*. (modifies *feathers*)
>
> He had a mood *to wreck every mellifluous conversation*. (modifies *mood*)

Adverb:

> I sent Satchmo a billet-doux *to tell him* about Julio.
>
> He was determined *to dazzle her*. (modifies *determined*)
>
> She was braced *to defy him*. (modifies *braced*)
>
> The sandman, in cahoots with the vampire, lays the subject *to rest*. (modifies *lays*)
>
> I am here *to take a look* as well as *to take a sunbath*. (modifies *here*)
>
> They organized an excursion *to discover the source of these rumors*. (modifies *organized*)
>
> Coming into a clearing in the forest that did not show on any map, they tilted their puzzled heads heavenward *to discover a corresponding tear in the sky*.
>
> She conjured up visions of unearthly buffoons *to while away her dread*. (modifies *conjured*)
>
> Who needs a net *to catch butterflies?* (modifies *needs*: in order to catch)

I am here to take a look as well as to take a sunbath.

This last is an offhand remark Mog Cinders made, flaunting her own free-spirited (and unencumbered-bodied) approach to the hunt, and so the phrase does belong to *needs* and is an adverb. But if the Girl Scout master is standing in the middle of the forest with his troop scattered hither and yon while he's trying to go by the book and proceed in an orderly fashion through the various requisite skills they must acquire, he would ask in the same words a different question: "Who needs a net *to catch butterflies*?" meaning that he has all these butterfly nets (i.e., nets to catch butterflies) and is bellowing his perfectly sincere question, to which he wants serious and eager responses (unlike Mog, whose question was rhetorical, and show-offish besides) so that the butterfly nets will wind up in the hands of all who need them—not just to catch butterflies, but to fulfill the afternoon's program. In this instance, then, the phrase *to catch butterflies* is acting as an adjective, modifying *net*—telling us what kind of net it is.

The same rigorous analysis could be applied to the excursion ("They organized an excursion *to discover the source of these rumors*")—but they've already departed, *in a boat* (adverb) *with a glass bottom* (adjective).

The following glimpse of the faun in an intimate, unguarded moment is composed almost entirely of phrases —so many it would be absurd to set them off in italics.

> How he loved to dangle his participles, brush
> his forelock off his forehead with his foreleg,
> and gaze into the aqueous depths.

There are really three infinitive phrases together, all riding on the same *to*: *to dangle . . .* , *to brush . . .* , *to gaze . . .* The prepositional phrases show the ways and means of these narcissistic gestures: *off his forehead, with his foreleg, into the aqueous depths.*

Participial Phrases:

Participial phrases, enamored of nouns and pronouns, subjects and objects, subjective and objective complements, wouldn't be caught dead with anything else. Functioning as adjectives, as *enamored* just did and *functioning* is here, they insinuate themselves into all points of a sentence and frequently find themselves misplaced — but we'll get to the amusement *provided by such juxtapositions** after *visiting them where they belong*.† You'll remember from the "Verbals" chapter that participles come in both past and present tenses, to name the simplest of their time zones. A participial phrase begins with one or the other and comes as close as it can to the word(s) it's describing. *Glancing at these sentences*, you'll refresh your memory about participles and recognize how often they come into your life — never alone, but with accomplices — to create phrases, which then form promiscuous attachments all over the written world.

The flasher loafing along the
sidelines was seized with a
fit of pudeur.

Present Participle:

The genius *lounging on the lawn* is my nemesis.
The ghost *leaning against the parapet* decided to
sally forth.
The flasher *loafing along the sidelines* was seized
with a fit of pudeur.
The physicist *shambling provocatively up to the
lectern* was a case of $E = mc^2$.

* *Provided by such juxtapositions* (participial phrase).

† *Visiting them where they belong* (gerund phrase as object of preposition).

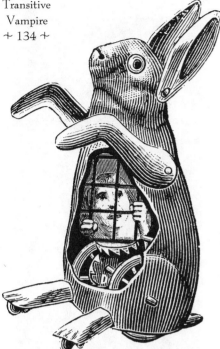

The rabbit ejected from the top
hat was a fake.

Past Participle:

> The rabbit *ejected from the top hat* was a fake.
> The starlet, *intoxicated by their cozy chat*, lit a cigar.
> *Battered by winds of misfortune*, Flaumina Untergasser's spring collection hobbled down the runway to the adagios of Fascist Italy.
> The cul-de-sac *encountered at the end of the road* contained a secret door.

Past and Present (and Past Perfect) Mingling, as they often do:

> The girl *squatting under the bridge* is a debutante.
> The troll *taking out his handkerchief* is visibly moved by her lament.
> The troll, *visibly moved by her lament*, is taking out his handkerchief.
> *Having run home to his mommy*, the gadfly was preparing for the coming critique.
> Jonquil, *anticipating Torquil's arrival*, strutted and fretted for an hour across this page.
> The bedroom, *suffused with a slovenly glow*, awaited their belated tryst.
> Torquil and Jonquil, *exhausted and turned inside out*, rang for lager and lobster claws.
> The baba *seated by the window* is swapping insults with Pythagoras.
> Her grandson, *engaged to that girl of serpentine charms*, is proposing a toast to her uncle.
> *Having shed our pelts in the entryway*, we stepped into a room ablaze with good cheer and *crackling with come-ons and quips*.
> The pelts, *shed and tossed into a muffled heap*, behaved with placid decorum while a cacophony of bestial bellowings proceeded in the adjoining room.

Muffled by the density of this arrangement, the
  pelts still managed to whisper among
  themselves about these disgraceful goings-on.
Rebuked by a bouncer / wearing spats, the persona
  non grata walked off with the revolting door.
That bear *stretching himself* in a flying nightgown
  is a member of the Chiroptera family.
Having lost all joy in life, Mucho Trabajo puts an
  ad in the personals *seeking cheap thrills* in his
  mistress's back lot.
Sophie, *abandoning her rented canoe*, exchanges
  pleasantries in the shade with a newt.

As in all the above examples, this last sentence contains a
participial phrase plus a couple of prepositional phrases:

in the shade
with a newt

That bear stretching himself in
a flying nightgown is a member
of the Chiroptera Family.

Gerund Phrases

Does the word *gerunds* produce a flutter of recognition, if not fondness, in your heart? We barely touched them in the "Verbals" chapter, where they showed us, in various contortions and upstanding examples, how a gerund, with its *-ing* ending, looks like a participle but, in fact, goes its separate way. That's because a gerund is a verbal noun and functions in all the ways that other nouns do. If you're confused in the presence of an *-ing* word, you can find out if it's a gerund by making it submit to this simple test (no torturing the prisoner, please): Can it be preceded by an article or by a possessive form?

> Alyosha's stroking gargoyles has quite done in her hands.
> The stroking, while not fatal, exacts a sacrifice of her flesh.

Go back and try it with the above instructions:

> you can find out if it's a gerund by *your making it* submit to this simple test

> none of *your torturing* the prisoner, please

> *the torturing* of your prisoner is not allowed

Here is one gerund, *ogling*, demonstrating its full spectrum of nounlike functions down at the docks:

> *Ogling stevedores* is his favorite lunch break. (subject)
> He relishes *ogling stevedores*. (direct object)
> A frequent pastime of his is *ogling stevedores*. (subjective complement)

He revels in *ogling stevedores*. (object of
    preposition *in*)
Ogling stevedores is his just dessert. (subject
    again)

But in

    Ogling stevedores, he forgot to look at his watch
        or watch the clock and missed an urgent
        appointment with his podiatrist,

ogling stevedores is a participial phrase modifying our
nameless voyeur.

    Ordering these lobster claws was a terrific idea.
    Eating them is even better.
    How about *following them up* with a bed of
        oysters?
    By *confessing her culpabilities*, she cleared the way
        for more. (gerund phrase as object of
        preposition)
    Through *measuring her fatal flaws*, he was able to
        predict her expenses.
    They got five years for *toting a gun*.
    Sprinkling sand at bedtime is a thankless
        profession. (*at bedtime* is a prepositional
        phrase here, modifying the subject of the
        sentence)
    What would her mother think of her *bawling her
        heart out* in the company of a scratchy old
        troll?

Absolute Phrases

An absolute phrase doesn't quite go along with the pack
— the way other phrases we've considered behave — because it is grammatically independent of the sentence
about which it has something to say. An absolute phrase
is made up of a participle combined with a noun or pronoun, and, functioning as an adjective, modifies an entire
sentence or clause.

> *The wine having been poisoned*, he convulsed.
> *The truth having slipped out*, she winked.
> *The night being eerie*, we quivered.
> *The baguette plundered*, they starved.
> Jonquil lay passed out on the veranda, *Torquil
> having popped the question.*
> The magician was out on his ear, *his chicanery
> having been unmasked.*
> *The sandman's footfalls still freshly retreating*, an
> apparition presents itself.
> *Things having proceeded as planned*, the rats were
> rubbing their paws on their lapels and looking
> very smug.

Noun and Verb Phrases

As if all this carrying on around the subject and predicate
weren't enough, *they* have clutched their own kinds of
phrases smack against their bosoms by calling the noun
plus its modifiers a noun phrase, and the main verb plus
its auxiliaries a verb phrase. The noun phrases you are
about to read contain prepositional phrases that modify
the subject, as is often the case.

Noun Phrase:

> *The four rats up on the roof* are unarmed.
> *The debutante with mud on her dress* was hauled in
>   on vagrancy charges.

Verb Phrase:

> She *has been persuaded* to repent.
> He *is being forced* to recant.
> We *have been invited* to watch.

❦ Clauses ❦

Phrases, as we've seen, can cut capers all over your sentences — and do so with neither subject nor predicate to animate, move, or brace them from within. Clauses, having more to say, are a different story. With both a subject and a predicate, a clause can even stand alone, conveying a complete thought as a part of a compound sentence, or comprising a simple sentence in itself. Independent clauses (the kind that can stand alone) and dependent, or subordinate, clauses find each other and move in together. A dependent, or subordinate, clause — in some cases quite a long one — acts as a part of speech, modifying or restricting the meaning of the main clause. Most sentences result from the combination, embrace, dance, pact between independent and dependent clauses. Were it not for this shapely symbiosis, the rhythms and relationships in our writing would be blunted and stunted, merely routine, belying the complex interplay that teases us and blazes the way through our lives and thoughts.

Even so, after all we've been through, clauses come as something of an anticlimax. They're so resolute and smug in their sense of completeness, and that also goes for the ones that strike a subordinate pose to attract a dominant thought — since they know perfectly well that by dropping a mere syllable or two, they *could* stand on their own. Even though a clause can be modified, most of its mind's made up. No wonder we dangle participles, shift our tenses, sunder our infinitives with gossip and quips, carry on in all directions before closing the sentence with a thud. Or, conversely, since it *does* know where it's going, why the dalliance, let's get to the point and beat it. All these fierce, sleepy, and madcap solutions will play tag further on, and that's the only incitement I can see to stick to the subject at hand.

Independent Clauses

An independent clause makes sense by itself and could make it as a separate sentence. It's more likely to be called an independent clause when it's part of a longer sentence. Two grammatically equivalent independent clauses may be linked by a coordinating conjunction like *and* or *but* or *or*:

> I fondled his lapel.
> I fondled his lapel, and I caressed his socks.

The independent clause *I fondled his lapel* stands alone in the first example and is joined by another independent clause, *I caressed his socks*, in the second.

> I ruffled his hair, and I beseeched him to relent.
> She was kicked by the soft shoe of destiny, and
>   she landed in Wales.
> The mannequin gave the baby vampire her
>   phone number, but she knew he'd never call.
> The tycoon snapped his avuncular suspenders,
>   and he called for another round.
> Her irony is getting rusty, and her audience is
>   bored.

He lifted her comatose toe in his palm, and he pronounced her over the scourge.

Those of you intrigued by the possibilities and relationships among clauses will find more to satisfy your curiosity in *The Well-Tempered Sentence*.

Dependent Clauses

A dependent clause needs the rest of the sentence (the independent, or main, clause) for the full impact of its meaning to be felt. Yes, it has both subject and verb, but it's gone too far to remain alone.

You could think of the linking word (usually a relative pronoun or subordinate conjunction) as a secondary sex characteristic its clause displays to attract, then hold, an independent, but bored and lonely, clause.

I fondled his lapel *before I caressed his socks.*
If she capitulates, we will reward her with a
   lollipop.
The debutante took to the great outdoors *as if
   she'd been raised by wolves.*
After the podiatrist pounced on her, he buffed her
   heels and tweaked her toes.
If this is love, I've made a terrible mistake.
If you'll let out the cat, I'll let out the last word.

It's the linking word that makes a clause dependent, that makes an independent clause necessary to create a complete sentence. A dependent clause can function as either an adjective or an adverb, as the previous examples have shown.

If this is love, I've made a
terrible mistake.

Adjective Clauses:
Adjective clauses are usually introduced by a relative pronoun: *who, whom, whose, whoever, whomever, that, which*.
Like a single-word adjective, such a clause modifies a
noun or pronoun.

> The dowager *who struck the match* was a
> pyromaniac.
> The hedonist *who was looking at his watch* began
> to scratch his crotch.

Everyone *who had a gripe* was gagged and bound
    at the door.
The Lilliputian *who was dressed in yellow silk* sang
    to her flea in its cage.
That beard, *which sits so awkwardly upon
    his face*, looks like a toupee for the
    temporomandibular joint.

Sometimes an adjective clause is introduced by *where*,
when, or *why*.

We've just about reached the point *where we
    usually roll our eyes upward and ask for heavenly
    succor.*

Adjective clauses can be more or less essential to the
identity of the nouns and pronouns they modify. When
a clause is intrinsic to what you're talking about, is as
much the point of the sentence as the subject or object
it's identifying or describing, it's called *restrictive*, since it
restricts the meaning, zeros in on specific qualities of this
noun or pronoun. When a clause is giving comparatively
incidental information, descriptive but not essential to
the point the sentence is making, it's called a *nonrestrictive* clause, and is set off by commas to further emphasize
its less important standing — and to it keep it out of the
way of the essential matter at hand.
    A variation of an earlier sentence illustrates what this
is all about:

There wasn't a single item in my closet *that
    would conform to the dress code*, nor was there a
    shoe fit to boogie in.

These clothes are along the lines of the Ancient Mari-
ner's "water, water, everywhere, nor any drop to drink."

The sentence is not about an empty closet, but about how unpresentable its contents were when held up to a cruel decree.

To further illuminate this issue, we'll take a silly example with one of this book's most improbable characters. Here the restrictive clause identifies the subject of the sentence.

The girl *who is stroking the gargoyle* is in love.

The adjective clause tells *which* girl is in love; there could be a dozen other girls engaged in equally ridiculous acts, but not with gargoyles.

A nonrestrictive clause gives descriptive information not strictly essential to the sentence.

Alyosha Luminosa, *who strokes gargoyles*, is in love.

Although the information in the clause may be interesting if it's the first time or two you've come across it, it isn't necessary for identifying this fetishist, whose unusual name is given.

Another way to express the difference is to say that nonrestrictive clauses are inclusive, rather than limiting, modifiers.

Now I'll turn you loose and let you see how insistently adjective clauses modify their partners in prose.

Restrictive:

The crawdads *that remain on their plates* could mean curtains for the cat.

Nonrestrictive:

The crawdads, *which were reduced to a scene of wanton devastation,* once creaked about a peaceable kingdom by the sea.

Restrictive:

The dahlias *that were left at the doorstep* may be of sinister intent.

Nonrestrictive:

The doorstep, *which belonged to a little girl with braces,* has withstood the delivery of some very odd bundles.

Restrictive:

The painting *that leered* was hauled into the judge's chambers and scolded.

Nonrestrictive:

The judge, *who had no children of his own,* chuckled as he imagined inviting it home to view his French postcard collection.

Restrictive:

The sorceress *who protects this island* is sorting out the mess at the schloss.

The frog *that's emerged from the samovar* was once a teen beauty queen.

Most contestants *who've shown great promise* have met with a similar end.

The cat *who's got the insouciant look in his eyes* is up to something good or evil.

That cat *who's checking out the back room* says he's here on a divine mission.

Those mastodons *that wear braces* should have stuck to the angel food.

The specter *that is lurching down the street* is my
pal.

The hand *that is languishing on the windowsill*
once was mine.

The marks *that are fading on my throat* are not
fresh.

The chair *that she chanced to sit in* was wearing
two pairs of boots.

Nonrestrictive:

The specter, *which lurched its way beyond my sight,*
gave out a piercing shriek.

The languishing hand, *which once was mine,*
applauded.

The marks, *which are not fresh,* were caused by
neither beast nor man.

The message, *which may have been an amorous
one,* was written in a feline hand.

That cat who's checking out the back room says he's here on a divine mission.

The little maestro, *who'd always had a thing for her*, turned the diva into a tenor and had his tailor take care of the rest.

The maestro's claque, *which follows him erratically*, is eating sherbet at the orchestra's expense.

Flaumina Untergasser, *who's a poet à la mode*, has a villa near the Malcontessa's.

Mog Cinders, *who's both an upright scholar and a grande horizontale*, is pursuing her studies in Nepal.

Her lederhosen, *which have seen better days as a cow*, stir with life when she sits on the grass.

As you may have noticed, *that* is ordinarily found leading into restrictive clauses, while *which* announces the arrival of clauses that are nonrestrictive.

Adverb Clauses:

An adverb clause behaves like a one-word adverb. Linking words, as we conceived them earlier, are attributes that dependent clauses flash or flutter to attract independent clauses into relationships with them, relationships that result in complex sentences. In adverb clauses, these seductive little words, which exercise such magnetic power, strike poses or express attitudes or intentions, the tunes to which the so-called independent clauses hop.

Cause:
as, because, inasmuch as, now that, since
Comparison:
as, as if, more than, rather than
Concession:
although, even if, even though, though

Condition:
but that, except that, if, if only, in case, provided that, unless, whether
Manner:
as, as if, as though
Place:
where, wherever
Purpose:
in order that, so, so that, that
Result:
so, that
Time:
after, as, as soon as, before, since, till, until, when, whenever, while

To recapitulate this mating dance between dependent and independent clauses as described in the "Words" chapter: Subordinate conjunctions usher or shove you right into a dependent clause. If a sentence begins with a dependent clause (as this one does), the subordinate conjunction (in this case, *if*) comes first, so that it can state the condition or circumstance modifying the independent clause. Otherwise a subordinate conjunction may come between the parts of the sentence it connects.

If Lucifer confesses, we'll let the rest of you go.
They dropped the subject *before it got too hot.*

Cause:
*Since the schloss lies far to the east of our mother
     tongues,* we always come with interpreters.
I've put a spell on you *because you could use a little
     control.*
I laughed *because I was miffed.*
I scowled, *since I was thrilled.*
He left *because he was perplexed.*

Thugs Bunny?

We made up, *since we were inseparable.*
My son is a horse thief *because his father was a thug.*

Comparison:

Her billowing voice is as voluminous *as a résumé of the wind.* (It is understood that *as a résumé of the wind is* is meant.)
She has strayed farther *than most lost sheep* [*have strayed*].
Her gullibility is more remarkable *than her sins* [*are*].

She has strayed farther than most lost sheep.

Concession:

He excoriated her behavior *even though he secretly approved.*
She swooned, *though there was a curious gleam in her eye.*
She stepped into the empty elevator, *although she'd already gone as far as she could.*

Condition:

If you spank me, I will comply.
Unless I am mistaken, we've already been through that.

If you should have any qualms about the coat hangers and bloomers, flash us a signal from the severed black oak.

If someone has a complaint, he's in for a bout with Sir Gallimauf.

Manner:

He bounced along in his checked suit *as if the world were his.*

Anjula took to the great outdoors *as if she'd been raised by wolves.*

Place:

We sought the truth *where it was least obvious.*

He followed her *wherever she ambled or rolled.*

He scratched her flesh *where he imagined it itched.*

Purpose:

She shuddered *in order that she might find relief.*

He whispered softly *so that she would draw nearer the fire.*

She took his comfort *that she might save it for later.*

Result:

He waxed so eloquent *that he made his point too soon.*

We were enfeebled by his cajolery, *so we left.*

Time:

I'll bring you back *before I take you away.*

After the podiatrist pounced on her, he buffed her heels and tweaked her toes.

When that cat purrs contentedly, it feels like the end of the world.

When that cat purrs contentedly, it feels like the end of the world.

Just lie here quietly *till we tell you to unwind and
move your arms like a clock's.*

Naturally, we'd prefer to take our tea in the
cloakroom *while the rest of you carry on in the
fountain in the dark.*

When you asked me if I wanted more, I thought
you were referring to coffee.

When I last saw him, in that sea-blue bus, he was
scattering glass beads behind him *as he fled.*

Here are some more examples of how adjective and adverb clauses behave on their own and in cahoots.

Those mastodons *that wear braces* are having
trouble with the marzipan.

The dentist *who was on call to reopen their mouths*
was summoned out of a sizzling tango.

As he tried to break free of his partner's embrace, he
suspected a mechanical failure.

Then there was a mouse *that had an intense desire
to meet the king of the rats, who lived in a large
bowl at the edge of the dessert.* To do so would
place his family in grave danger, *for they were
sworn to uphold their honor by shunning lowly
rodents and vermin*, royalty and all.

But no matter! *Whatever his mother and
handkerchief-wringing sisters would say*, pleading
and writhing all over the family room and
kicking pillows into his face, our would-be
hero had his sights set on the bucktoothed
princess with her long silky tail.

Noun Clauses:

A noun clause gets around in the same way that a noun
or pronoun does. To be subordinate, it's introduced by

one of the relative pronouns: *who, whom, whose, which* (and their *-ever* forms: *whoever, whomever, whichever*), *that*, or by *when, where, why, how,* or *whether.*

> I believe *that we've met before.* (direct object)
> I bet you say that to *whoever catches your fancy or changes your face across a crowded room.* (object of preposition)
> *That we've met before* is an impossibility. (subject)
> *That we've met again* is a miracle! (subject)
> His preposterous delusion is *that we've met before.* (subjective complement)
> This delusion of his, *that we've met before,* must not come between us now. (appositive)
> Our earlier acquaintance, or shall I say intimacy, goes back to *when you were on the skids and guzzling muscatel.* (object of preposition)
> I don't make a habit of giving *whoever claims our previous friendship* my phone number. (indirect object)

That is another of those words that may sometimes be safely omitted, but is still understood grammatically.

Clauses and Classification

Are you not shocked, stunned, staggered, or stilettoed to hear from these very fingertips that sentences have been classified? I've put it off for as long as I could, taking detours through the minutest considerations, dallying among the lycanthropes in "Agreements," having a tea party with the mastodons in "Phrases," but after all those close calls, catcalls, and house calls, we must face the inevitable: even sentences have names. It's been just ducky not knowing them; in another page or two we can all pretend I never mentioned them.

Every grammatically complete sentence (except for the verbless sentence, or a sentence with subject or verb understood) has at least one independent clause. The four kinds of sentences are: *simple*, *compound*, *complex*, and *compound-complex*.

Any sentence, however long or short, that has a single subject and a single predicate is a *simple sentence* — but any part of the single clause making up the sentence may be compound.

> The lithium worked.

The *compound sentence* has two or more independent clauses.

> The lithium worked, and the mania subsided.
> The lithium worked, the mania subsided, and
> the depression lifted.

The *complex sentence* has one independent clause and one or more dependent clauses.

> As the lithium took effect, the mania subsided.

The *compound-complex sentence* is a compound sentence with one or more dependent clauses.

> As the lithium took effect, the mania subsided
> and the depression lifted.

Fragments, Splices, ❧ and Run-ons ❧

Fragments

Within the leaps and boundaries of this book, a handful of words tossed onto the table may be alluring, soporific, banal, or breathtaking — may even tickle your antipodes — but in most cases, if it's missing a subject and predicate, or includes a subordinate clause with nothing to complete it, it's a fragment trying to masquerade as a sentence. Sentence fragments can add a needed change in rhythm, can mimic thinking out loud, can effectively imply the missing half, which is sometimes louder by its absence. When all these enhancements fail to come across, though, the fragment should be allowed to join a well-endowed (independent) clause to create a complete statement, question, thought — or be rewritten to do so all by itself. The latter option can often be realized through the mere removal of the subordinate conjunction that's made it an unattached subordinate clause — and, voilà, a complete sentence that defies all Procrustean curmudgeons to knock it down. Familiarity with phrases and clauses can guide you through this labyrinth, even change its very shape.

A flashback to the chapter "Words" flashes us forward to this point. Remember? Since a subordinate conjunction at the beginning of a clause renders it unable to stand alone (as the word *since* does in this one), and since without the conjunction it would be just fine all by itself, you should be alert to the danger of sentence fragments so easily created by your failing to connect the dependent clause thus established to an accompanying independent clause. Relative pronouns, too, signal a dependent clause longing to join its mate: pronouns like *who, which, whom, that,* and *whose.* Among the subordinate conjunctions that might indicate a need for completion are: *after, although, as if, as long as, because, before, even though, even that, if, if only, in case, in order that, now that, since, that, though, till, unless, until, when, whenever, where, whereas,* and *while.*

Mere phrases sometimes come off as fragments, without the ample population and almost-subject-predicate profile of the typical dependent clause.

Fragment:

I was wasted. Having paced the floorboards twenty nights in a row. (possible solutions: linking participial phrase to the main clause; adding subordinate conjunction to show connection)

Sentence:

Having paced the floorboards twenty nights in a row, I was wasted.

Sentence:

I was wasted, having paced the floorboards twenty nights in a row.

Sentence:

I was wasted, since I'd paced the floorboards twenty nights in a row.

Sentence:

Since I'd paced the floorboards twenty nights in a row, I was wasted.

Fragment:
A shade of green which caught her eye.
Sentence:
A shade of green caught her eye.

Fragment:
Sometimes bras and panties would cry out to her to touch them. Navigating her way through the boutique.
Sentence:
Sometimes bras and panties would cry out to her to touch them as she navigated her way through the boutique.

Fragment:
The vampire scratched his head thoughtfully. As he bent over his conundrum.
Sentence:
The vampire scratched his head thoughtfully as he bent over his conundrum.

Fragment:
I want more. Because I'm one of those insatiable robots, you know.
Sentence:
I want more, because I'm one of those insatiable robots, you know.

Fragment:
Tripping over the ripped linoleum. She was floored.
Sentence:
Tripping over the ripped linoleum, she was floored.

Fragment:
Four ushers from the cinema, a small person with enormous eyes, a house cat on heroin — all of whom stranded in the cloakroom long after the concert among the querulous gestures of abandoned wraps.

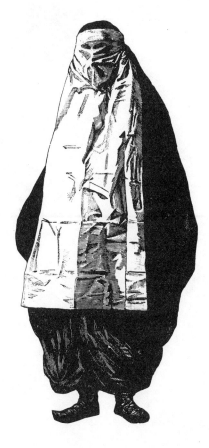

Sometimes bras and panties would cry out to her to touch them as she navigated her way through the boutique.

Sentence:

Four ushers from the cinema, a small person with enormous eyes, a house cat on heroin — all of them were stranded in the cloakroom long after the concert among the querulous gestures of abandoned wraps.

Sentence:

Among the querulous gestures of abandoned wraps long after the concert's end were four ushers from the cinema, a small person with enormous eyes, and a house cat on heroin.

Fragment:

We never arrived. The upshot being that we upset a bunch of excitable, expectant aunts and uncles.

S
E
N
T
E
N
C
E
S

We never arrived, with the upshot that we upset a bunch of excitable, expectant aunts and uncles.

We never arrived, which upset a bunch of excitable, expectant aunts and uncles.

Upsetting a bunch of excitable aunts and uncles, we never did arrive.

By not arriving, we upset a bunch of excitable, expectant aunts and uncles.

Fragment:

That samovar wasn't here yesterday. When I was calming down the wraps and cloaks with Gabor.

S   That samovar wasn't here yesterday when I was
E   calming down the wraps and cloaks with Gabor.

N   When I was calming down the wraps and cloaks
T   yesterday with Gabor, that samovar wasn't here.
E
N   That samovar wasn't here when I was calming
C   down the wraps and cloaks with Gabor yesterday.
E
S

Fragment:

Vague tremors disturbed the room. Which were small
and were caused by the electrical storm in the curtains.

Sentence:

The vague tremors disturbing the room were small and
were caused by the electrical storm in the curtains.

Fragment:

The lamia put the frog in her samovar. Which is where
she kept the false eyelashes and faux pearls.

S   The lamia put the frog in her samovar, with her
E   false eyelashes and faux pearls.

N   Her samovar, holding her false eyelashes and
T   faux pearls, is where the lamia put the frog.
E

N   The lamia put the frog in her samovar, usually
C   the place for her false eyelashes and pearls.

E   The lamia put the frog in her samovar, the usual
S   place for her false eyelashes and fake jewels.

Comma Splices and Run-ons

Two independent clauses sometimes try to cohabit a sentence, and, to lend a touch of decorum for their mothers, the neighbors, or a Green Card, slip a sliver of a comma between them — without the necessary link of a coordinating conjunction. And yet, as if to acknowledge that this comma weren't decorum enough, they often invite another word to come between them, as a chaperon — such as *this*, *another*, *there*, or *it* — to begin the second clause.

Instead of a comma, a period or semicolon will make sense of this coupling.

Possible solutions:
Insert a semicolon between the two independent clauses — especially when they are closely related; separate them with a period, making two complete sentences; summon a subordinate conjunction to link the thus-created dependent clause with the independent, or main, clause

Splice:
One type of protagonist is looking for himself at the bottom of every river, another type is looking for love.
Sentence:
One type of protagonist is looking for himself at the bottom of every river; another type is looking for love.
Sentence:
While one type of protagonist is looking for himself at the bottom of every river, another type is looking for love.

Splice:
They had a fatal attraction, it was based on *The Myth of Sisyphus* and a love of Harpo Marx.

Sentence:
They had a fatal attraction; it was based on *The Myth of Sisyphus* and a love of Harpo Marx.

Splice:
One way to find a sweetheart is to put an ad in the paper, another is to wait and see what the cat drags in.
Sentence:
One way to find a sweetheart is to put an ad in the paper; another is to wait and see what the cat drags in.

Splice:
She wrapped herself up in an enigma, there was no other way to keep warm.
Sentence:
She wrapped herself up in an enigma; there was no other way to keep warm.

Splice:
Little fauns are stroked on their haunches when they become too raucous, this calms their frisky young nerves.
Sentence:
Little fauns are stroked on their haunches when they become too raucous. This calms their frisky young nerves.

There are instances in which a comma should be used instead of a semicolon. When the clauses are concise and similar in construction or when the sentence has a casual lilt, use a comma between the clauses.

> I could hardly believe my senses, he so relieved my fever.
> She darkened his door, he lit her fire, they both burned.
> Have gun, will travel.

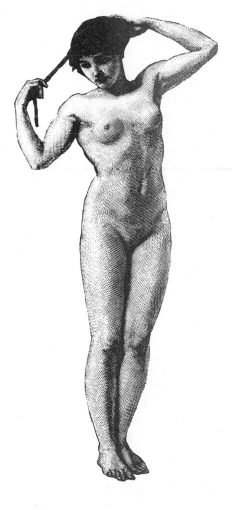

She wrapped herself up in an
enigma; there was no other
way to keep warm.

Joining two independent clauses with a conjunctive adverb can also produce a comma splice. The conjunctive
adverbs that especially deserve your suspicion are:

> accordingly, afterwards, also, besides,
> consequently, earlier, hence, however, later,
> moreover, nevertheless, otherwise, still, then,
> therefore, thus

These words express relationships between two clauses
or sentences, such as condition, time, contrast, accumu-
lation, and cause and effect. Subordinate conjunctions,
on the other hand, make a graceful link, while conveying
similar rapport.

Splice:
The intruders never failed to arrive with bonbons and
champagne, hence they were always welcome at the
schloss.

S
E
N
T
E
N
C
E
S

> The intruders never failed to arrive with bonbons
> and champagne. Hence, they were always wel-
> come at the schloss.

> The intruders never failed to arrive with bonbons
> and champagne, so they were always welcome at
> the schloss.

Splice:
The grandee bought himself a pair of roller skates, ac-
cordingly he rolled down the avenida in his shirtsleeves
with an unsteadiness unbecoming to his rank.
Sentence:
The grandee bought himself a pair of roller skates. Ac-

cordingly, he rolled down the avenida in his shirtsleeves with an unsteadiness unbecoming to his rank.

   Splice:
The angels are dancing the sarabande on the head of a pin, afterwards they'll cool their heels in the River Styx.
   Sentence:
The angels are dancing the sarabande on the head of a pin. Afterwards they'll cool their heels in the River Styx.

Run-ons

The parts of a run-on, or "fused" sentence, share the same underlying misconception about their relationship as do splices. They throw all caution and self-censorship to the winds, and lie together in a bed they've made with no comma, semicolon, period, *or* linking word. Any of the examples above could be turned into a run-on.

   They had a fatal attraction it was based on *The Myth of Sisyphus* and a love of Harpo Marx.

Here's a fresh new blunder:

   Run-on:
Her poise and panache are disconcerting they bring out the beast in me.
   Sentence:
Her poise and panache are disconcerting: they bring out the beast in me.

A Procrustean bed?

What a darling hat! It makes
your eyes bug out.

And another, more public one:

Run-on:
The audience coughed concordantly it had a cold in its
community chest.
Sentence:
The audience, sharing a community chest cold, coughed
concordantly.
Sentence:
With a cold in its community chest, the audience
coughed concordantly.

Run-on:
What a darling hat it makes your eyes bug out.
Sentence:
What a darling hat. It makes your eyes bug out.

Beyond Comma Splices

Here our approach with comma-spliced sentences tumbles us into a more sumptuous diversity, each rewrite becoming a new version, really, since the relationships don't remain exactly the same. Other arrangements and linking words bring changes in tone and meaning, set new dramas spinning, and let new words loose upon a page yet to be filled.

Not:
Torquil and Jonquil plotted their tryst, they gave it some furniture and an odd new twist.
But:
Torquil and Jonquil, plotting their tryst, gave it some furniture and an odd new twist.

Or:

With some furniture and an odd new twist, Torquil and Jonquil plotted their tryst.

Not:

Hey, girlie, drag your carcass over here, I wanna hold your hand!

But:

Hey, girlie, drag your carcass over here cuz I wanna hold your hand!

Or:

Hey, girlie, since I wanna hold your hand, bring the rest of you, too!

Not:

There are unbeaten paths she longs to prowl, for instance, the one that forks off early from the road to perdition.

But:

There are unbeaten paths she longs to prowl — for instance, the one that forks off early from the road to perdition.

Or:

Among the unbeaten paths she long to prowl is the one that forks off early from the road to perdition.

Or:

Among the unbeaten paths she longs to prowl is the one forking off early from the road to perdition.

Not:

The debutante was arraigned and scrubbed with harsh soap, they charged her with lurking with intent to loiter and with wearing her accessories to a crime.

But:

➤ After a harsh scrubbing with soap, the debutante, arraigned, was charged with lurking with intent to loiter and with wearing her accessories to a crime.

Or:

➤ After arraigning her and scrubbing her with harsh soap, they charged the debutante with lurking and loitering, and with wearing her accessories to a crime.

Or:

➤ At her arraignment, the debutante, thoroughly scrubbed with harsh soap, was charged with lurking with intent to loiter and with wearing her accessories to a crime.

Not:

The orgy proceeded parliamentarily, it began with banging the gavel and the minutes of the previous revels.

But:

➤ The orgy, proceeding parliamentarily, began with banging the gavel and the minutes of the previous revels.

Or:

➤ The orgy proceeded parliamentarily. It began with banging the gavel and the minutes of the previous revels.

Or:

➤ Gavel-banging and minutes-reading opened the orgy, which followed parliamentary procedures.

❦ Follow the Flight ❦

Follow the flight if you're wondering . . .

. . . why the debutante was considered a prime suspect in the murder of the pizza chef.

. . . if the accessories she was wearing were heisted from the samovar.

. . . about the father of Mog Cinders's daughter, Blaze.

. . . what was the name of the river.

. . . about other pursuits of the faun.

. . . what becomes of the baby vampire and what he does to his nanny.

. . . what a cow was doing in the powder room during the opera, and which opera it was.

. . . why the quintet hijacked the plane, and where to.

. . . if Alyosha ever publishes her studies of alchemy and Gothic cathedrals.

. . . about the relation between the pale horse/pale rider and the imprisoned protagonist.

. . . if Procrustean grammarians eat crustaceans, and if large and mysterious cats eat Procrustean grammarians.

. . . what was found in Gabor's cello case when it came through customs in Ljubljana.

❧ Illustration Credits ❧

The illustrations in this book were created from images in the following sources.

Thomas Bewick: *Vignettes.* Copyright © 1978 by The Scolar Press.

George Bruce's Son and Company: *Victorian Frames, Borders and Cuts.* Copyright © 1976 by Dover Publications, Inc.

Gustave Doré: *The Doré Illustrations for Dante's Divine Comedy.* Copyright © 1976 by Dover Publications, Inc.

Jean-Ignace-Isidore Gérard (Grandville): *Fantastic Illustrations of Grandville.* Copyright © 1974 by Dover Publications, Inc.

Konrad Gesner: *Curious Woodcuts of Fanciful and Real Beasts.* Copyright © 1971 by Dover Publications, Inc.

Carol Belanger Grafton: *Love and Romance.* Copyright © 1989 by Dover Publications, Inc.

Jim Harter: *Animals.* Copyright © 1979 by Dover Publications, Inc.

Jim Harter: *Harter's Picture Archive for Collage and Illustration.* Copyright © 1978 by Dover Publications, Inc.

Jim Harter: *Men: A Pictorial Archive from Nineteenth-Century Sources.* Copyright © 1980 by Dover Publications, Inc.

Jim Harter: *Women: A Pictorial Archive from Nineteenth-Century Sources.* Copyright © 1978 by Dover Publications, Inc.

Johann Georg Heck: *The Complete Encyclopedia of Illustration.* Copyright © 1979 by Park Lane, Crown Publishers, Inc.

🕯 Index 🕯

❦ About the Author ❦

KAREN ELIZABETH GORDON is the author of *The New Well-Tempered Sentence*, *The Ravenous Muse*, *The Red Shoes and Other Tattered Tales*, *The Disheveled Dictionary*, *Paris Out of Hand: A Wayward Guide*, and *Torn Wings and Faux Pas*. She divides her time between Berkeley, California, and France.